MW01412715

The Neocatechumenal Way

Neocatechumenale Iter

Statuta

Neocatechumenal Way

Statute

Hope Publishing House
Pasadena, California

Statute
of the
Neocatechumenal Way

Edited by:

Kiko Argüello
Carmen Hernández
F. Mario Pezzi

with the permission of the Pontifical Council for the Laity

Hope Publishing House
Pasadena, California

Copyright © 2003 The Family of Nazareth Foundation

All rights reserved.

For information address:

Hope Publishing House
P.O. Box 60008
Pasadena, CA 91116 - U.S.A.
Tel: (626) 792-6123 / Fax: (626) 792-2121
E-mail: hopepub@sbcglobal.net
Web site: http://www.hope-pub.com

Printed on acid-free paper

Library of Congress Cataloging-in-Publication Data

Neocatechumenale iter statuta. English.
    Statute of the Neocatechumenal way / Kiko Argüello, Carmen Hernández, Mario Pezzi, editors. – 1st American English ed.
    p. cm.
    ISBN 0-932727-99-9 (alk. paper)
    1. Neocatechumenate (Movement) I. Argüello, Kiko, 1939- II. Hernández, Carmen, 1936- III. Pezzi, Mario, 1942- IV. Title.
    BX809.N46 N4613
    271'.095–dc21

2003004605

Contents

	Introduction	viii
Part I –	The Decree of Approval and the Statute of the Neocatechumenal Way	
1 –	The Decree of Approval of the Statute of the Neocatechumenal Way	3
2 –	Statute of the Neocatechumenal Way	7
Part II –	Papal Discourse	
3 –	John Paul II: "The Statute: A Clear and Sure Rule of Life"	47
Part III –	Commentaries on the Day of Approval	
4 –	Address by Kiko Argüello	55
5 –	Address by Carmen Hernández	59
6 –	Address by Fr. Mario Pezzi	65
7 –	Address by Card. James Francis Stafford	67
8 –	Address of Card. James Francis Stafford's to the Itinerant Catechists	71
Part IV –	Juridical and Ecclesial Commentaries on the *Statute*	
9 –	Historical Notes *by Ezechiele Pasotti*	81
10 –	Canonical Observations on the *Statute of the Neocatechumenal Way* by Prof. Juan Ignacio Arrieta	87
11 –	Canonical Observations by Dr. Adelchi Chinaglia	95
12 –	Rediscovery of the Catechumenate and the Approval of the Neocatechumenal Way by Giuseppe Gennarini . .	102
Appendices		
I –	John Paul II: Letter *"Ogniqualvolta"*	113
II –	John Paul II: Letter *"È per me motivo..."*	116
III –	John Paul II: "Called to a Special Missionary Commitment"	118
IV –	John Paul II: Letter to Card. James Francis Stafford	122
V –	Congregation for Divine Worship: Note on the Neocatechumenal Communities (1974)	124

Introduction

Pope John XXIII, in the Apostolic Constitution "*Humanae salutis*" (1961), with which he convoked the Council, begins by saying: "*Today the Church is witnessing a crisis underway within society. While humanity is on the edge of a new era tasks of immense gravity and amplitude await the Church, as in the most tragic periods of history. It is a question in fact of bringing the modern world into contact with the vivifying and perennial energies of the Gospel*" (n. 2).

The Holy Spirit, which enlivens and guides the Church, brought about the Second Vatican Council to respond to this "*crisis underway*" of which the Pope speaks: the restoration of the Word of God (*Dei Verbum*), the reform of the Liturgy (*Sacrosanctum Concilium*), a new ecclesiology, the Church as body and sacrament of salvation (*Lumen Gentium*) – all this in function of its mission (*Gaudium et Spes*) to evangelize and save contemporary man.

In 1974, ten years after the birth of the Neocatechumenal Way in the shantytown, Pope Paul VI received us in an audience, along with pastors and catechists who were meeting in Rome, and said to us: "*To live and foster this re-awakening is what you call a kind of 'post-baptism', which can renew in our contemporary Christian communities the effects of maturity and depth which were achieved in the early Church during the period of preparation before Baptism. You do this afterwards. Whether 'before' or 'after' is secondary, I would say. The fact is that you aim at the authenticity, fullness, coherence and sincerity of Christian life. And this is a very great merit, which, I repeat, consoles us enormously...*" (*Notitiae*, n. 95-96, July-August 1974, p. 230).

On August 30, 1990, Pope John Paul II, in the letter *Ogniqualvolta* (AAS 82 [1990], 1513-1515), addressed to Mgr. Paul Josef Cordes, then Vice-president of the Pontifical Council for the Laity and charged *ad personam* with the apostolate of the Neocatechumenal Communities, recognizes the Neocatechumenal Way as "*an itinerary of Catholic formation valid for our society and for our times*" and expresses the wish that "*the Brothers in the Episcopate – together with their presbyters – value and help this work for the new evangelization so that it may be implemented according to the lines proposed by its initiators, in the spirit of service to the local Ordinary and in communion with him in the context of the unity of the local Church and the universal Church.*"

Later, on January 24, 1997, the Holy Father himself invited us to proceed with the work of drawing up "a Statute of the Way, ... *a very important step, which opens the way to a formal juridical recognition by the Church, giving a further guarantee of the authenticity of your charism.*"

Witnesses of how much the Lord has worked in more than 30 years of the way, with the help of a team of brothers, the assistance of some canon lawyers and under the guidance of the Pontifical Council for the Laity, we undertook this work of drawing up the text of the *Statute*, seeking to be faithful to the gift received and to the praxis of the Neocatechumenal Communities as it has taken shape during all these years in many countries throughout the world.

In these pages we are happy to present the *Decree of Approval of the Neocatechumenal Way* and the text of the *Statute*, dated June 29, 2002, solemnity of the holy Apostles Peter and Paul.

In our opinion there are two new important things in this Statute.

Above all, the approval of the Neocatechumenal Way as a post-baptismal catechumenate, a Christian initiation, an instrument which the Holy See offers to the Bishops so that, in response to modern atheism, the Baptism of Christians can be strengthened; but it also offers the possibility of a baptismal catechumenate for those who are not yet baptized. With this *Statute*, the Pope offers to the Bishops and the Episcopal conferences a means of Christian initiation to implement the New Evangelization in the face of secularization.

The second novelty of great importance, especially in the deconstructed society in which the man of today lives, is that this post-baptismal catechumenate offers the possibility of living a permanent education in the faith in small communities, thus re-connecting with the life and pastoral experience of the Church of the first centuries. At that time, Christians were inserted into living communities, and thanks to a faith which had been assessed in a serious catechumenate, they were able to show to a pagan world the signs of the new man of which the Sermon on the Mount speaks, the man who *loves the enemy as Christ has loved us,* signs which, little by little, converted the Roman Empire.

In order for this love, which is the nature of God himself, to be visible today to everyone as the sacrament which gives salvation, a way to grow in our faith is needed — a post-baptismal catechumenate such as the Neocatechumenal Way described in this Statute.

—*Kiko Argüello*
—*Carmen Hernández*
—*Father Mario Pezzi*

Rome, August 15, 2002
Solemnity of the Assumption of the Blessed Virgin Mary

Part I

The Decree of Approval and the Statute of the Neocatechumenal Way

1

The Decree of Approval of the Statute of the Neocatechumenal Way

The Neocatechumenal Way began in 1964 in the slums of Palomeras Altas, Madrid, through the work of Mr. Francisco (Kiko) Argüello and Ms. Carmen Hernández who, at the request of the poor with whom they were living, began to proclaim to them the Gospel of Jesus Christ. As time passed, this *kerygma* was embodied in a catechetical synthesis, founded on the tripod: "Word of God – Liturgy – Community," that seeks to lead people to fraternal communion and mature faith.

This new catechetical experience, born in the wake of the renewal inspired by the Second Vatican Council, attracted the keen interest of Archbishop Casimiro Morcillo, then Archbishop of Madrid, who encouraged the initiators of the Way to spread it to those parishes who asked for it. This experience of evangelization thus spread gradually through the archdiocese of Madrid and to other Spanish dioceses.

In 1968, the initiators of the Neocatechumenal Way arrived in Rome and settled in the Borghetto Latino. With the permission of Cardinal Angelo Dell'Acqua, then vicar-general of His Holiness for the city and district of Rome, the first catechesis began in the parish of Our Lady of the Blessed Sacrament and the Canadian Martyrs. Since then, the Way has continued to spread to dioceses around the world and even to mission countries.

The Neocatechumenal Way is at the service of the Bishops and parish priests as an itinerary for the rediscovery of Baptism and an ongoing education in the faith, offered to the faithful who want to revive in their lives the riches of Christian initiation by travelling this path of conversion and catechesis. As the Holy Father wrote, in this process an important help can be offered by "a post-baptismal catechesis in the form of the catechumenate by presenting again some elements from the 'Rite of the Christian Initiation of Adults' with the purpose of allowing a person to grasp and live the immense and extraordinary richness and responsibility of the Baptism he has received" (*Christifideles laici* n. 61).

The Way–whose itinerary is lived in parishes and in small communities made up of people of different ages and social conditions–has the ultimate goal of gradually bringing the faithful to intimacy with Jesus Christ, making them active subjects of the Church and credible witnesses of the Good News of our Savior everywhere. The Neocatechumenal Way is also an instrument for the Christian initiation of adults who are preparing themselves to receive Baptism.

The actual practice of the Way follows the guidelines contained in the Catechetical Directory–*The Neocatechumenal Way, Guidelines for the Teams of Catechists* (cf. *Statute*, art. 2.2), subject to the joint approval of the Congregations for the Doctrine of the Faith, for the Clergy and for Divine Worship and the Discipline of the Sacraments.

At different times and in different ways, the Holy Father has addressed the Neocatechumenal Way stressing the abundant fruits of Gospel radicalism and the extraordinary missionary zeal that the Way brings to the life of the lay faithful, to families, to parish communities, AND the wealth of vocations it inspires to the priestly and religious life, proving to be an "itinerary of Catholic formation, valid for our society and our time" (AAS 82 [1990] 1513-1515).

In the audience granted to the initiators and directors of the Neocatechumenal Way from around the world on January 24, 1997, on the occasion of the commemoration of the 30 years of life of the Way, the Holy Father expressly urged the drafting of the Statute as, "a very important step that will open the way to the formal juridical recognition by the Church, and giving you a further guarantee of the authenticity of your charism" (Address to the Neocatechumenal Way, *L'Oss. Rom.*, Jan. 25, 1997, p. 4; ORE, Feb. 5, 1997, p. 9).

From that moment, accompanied by the Pontifical Council for the Laity, the initiators began the process of elaborating a set of norms that would enable them to regulate the practice and integrate the Neocatechumenal Way into the ecclesial framework.

On April 5, 2001, in an autograph addressed to Cardinal James Francis Stafford, President of the Pontifical Council for the Laity, the Supreme Pontiff, while reiterating his request, reconfirmed this Council's competence to approve the Statute of the Neocatechumenal Way and entrusted to its competence the future guidance of the Way (cf. Letter to Cardinal Francis Stafford, 5 April 2001; ORE, May 2, 2001, p. 5).

And so:

Taking into account the numerous spiritual fruits that the practice of the Neocatechumenal Way – whose existence has been accepted and appreciated in many local churches for more than 30 years – has contributed to the new evangelization and which have been reported to the Pontifical Council for the Laity by many letters of recommendation of Cardinals, Patriarchs and Bishops;

After careful examination of the text of the Statute – the result of a laborious process of collaboration between the initiators of the Neocatechumenal Way and the Pontifical Council for the Laity who were able to take advantage of the contribution made by the different departments of the Roman Curia, each within its own sphere of competence;

Taking note of the request sent to this Council on April 5, 2002, by Mr. Francisco (Kiko) Argüello, Ms. Carmen Hernández and Fr. Mario Pezzi, members of the international leadership team of the Neocatechumenal Way, asking the Council to expedite the approval of the Statute of the Neocatechumenal Way;

Relying on articles 131 and 133, 1 and 2, of the Apostolic Constitution *Pastor Bonus* on the Roman Curia, the Pontifical Council for the Laity

Decrees

the approval *ad experimentum* for a period of five years of the Statute of the Neocatechumenal Way, as duly authenticated by the Council, of which a copy must be deposited in the archives of the Council. This is done with the confidence that the approved Statute offer firm and secure guidelines for the life of the Way and are an important aid for pastors in their fatherly and careful accompaniment of the neocatechumenal communities.

Granted at the Vatican on June 29, 2002, Solemnity of Sts. Peter and Paul, Apostles, Patrons of the City of Rome.

James Francis Card. Stafford, *President*
Stanisław Ryłko, *Secretary*

From *L'Osservatore Romano,* English Edition, July 31, 2002

STATUTE OF THE NEOCATECHUMENAL WAY

INDEX

Title I: **Nature and implementation of the Neocatechumenal Way**
    Art. 1: Nature of the Neocatechumenal Way
    Art. 2: Implementation of the Neocatechumenal Way
    Art. 3: Tasks of the international Responsible Team of the Way
    Art. 4: Temporal Goods

Title II: **Neocatechumenal or post-baptismal catechumenate**
    Chapter I: Fundamental Elements of the Neocatechumenate
    Art. 5: Recipients
    Art. 6: The Neocatechumenate implemented in the parish
    Art. 7: The Neocatechumenate implemented in small communities
    Art. 8: Initial catecheses, neocatechumenal itinerary, "tripod" and team of catechists
    Chapter II: Initial Catecheses
    Art. 9: Kerygma and celebrations
    Art. 10: Birth of the neocatechumenal communities
    Chapter III: Word, Liturgy and Community
      Section 1: *Word of God*
      Art. 11: Weekly celebration of the Word

Section 2: *Liturgy*
- Art. 12: Paschal Vigil
- Art. 13: Eucharist
- Art. 14: Penance, prayer, liturgical year, practices of piety

Section 3: *Community*
- Art. 15: Community dimension and *convivence*
- Art. 16: The experience of *koinonia* and the fruits of the community
- Art. 17: Missionary initiation
- Art. 18: Vocational initiation

Chapter IV: The neocatechumenal itinerary: phases, steps and passages
- Art. 19: 1st phase: post-baptismal pre-catechumenate
- Art. 20: 2nd phase: post-baptismal catechumenate
- Art. 21: 3rd phase: rediscovery of the election

Title III: Ongoing education in faith – a way of renewal in the parish

- Art. 22: Ongoing education in the small community
- Art. 23: A way of renewal in the parish

Title IV: Baptismal Catechumenate

- Art. 24: Catechumens
- Art. 25: Neophytes

Title V: Form of service to the catechesis

- Art. 26: Diocesan Bishop
- Art. 27: Pastors and presbyters
- Art. 28: Catechists
- Art. 29: Formation of catechists
- Art. 30: Neocatechumenal Center
- Art. 31: Itinerant catechists
- Art. 32: Itinerant presbyters
- Art. 33: Families in mission

Title VI: International Responsible Team of the Way

- Art. 34: Current international Responsible Team of the Way
- Art. 35: Election of the international Responsible Team of the Way

Final disposition

STATUTE OF THE NEOCATECHUMENAL WAY

Title I

Nature and implementation of the Neocatechumenal Way

Article 1
[Nature of the Neocatechumenal Way]

§ 1. The nature of the Neocatechumenal Way is defined by His Holiness John Paul II when he writes: *"I recognize the Neocatechumenal Way as an itinerary of Catholic formation, valid for our society and for our times."*[1]

§ 2. The Neocatechumenal Way is at the service of the Bishops as a form of diocesan implementation of Christian initiation and of ongoing education in faith, in accordance with the indications of the Second Vatican Council[2] and the Magisterium of the Church.[3]

---

[1] JOHN PAUL II, Epist. *Ogniqualvolta*, 30 August 1990, *AAS* 82 (1990) 1515.

[2] "The catechumenate for adults, comprising several distinct steps, is to be restored" (VATICAN II, *Sacrosanctum Concilium*, 64); cf. ibid., *Ad Gentes*, 13-14.

[3] Following the Conciliar Decrees, the Sacred Congregation for Divine Worship published the *Ordo Initiationis Christianae Adultorum* (RCIA). Chapter IV of the RCIA suggests the adapted use of catechesis and of some rites belonging to the catechumenate for the conversion and maturation in the faith of baptized adults.

As a result, the Magisterium has reiterated several times the necessity and urgency of a "post-baptismal catechumenate." Cf. especially:

–PAUL VI, Ap. Ex. *Evangelii Nuntiandi*, 44: "By now it is clear that contemporary conditions make it ever more urgent that catechetical instruction is given in the form of a catechumenate."

–JOHN PAUL II, Ap. Ex. *Catechesi Tradendæ*, 44: "Our pastoral and missionary concern ... is for those who, even if born in a Christian country, even in a sociologically Christian context, have never been educated in their faith and, as adults, are true catechumens."

–JOHN PAUL II, Ap. Ex. *Christifideles Laici*, 61: "A help [in the formation of Christians] may be given ... through a post-baptismal catechesis of a catechumenate kind, by means of re-proposing some elements of the Rite of Christian Initiation of Adults aimed at leading to the acceptance and living of the immense and extraordinary riches and responsibilities of one's Baptism."

§ 3. The Neocatechumenal Way is composed of an ensemble of spiritual goods:

1st. The "Neocatechumenate,"[4] or post-baptismal catechumenate, according to the form described in Title II;

2nd. The ongoing education in faith, according to the form described in Title III;

3rd. The baptismal catechumenate, according to the form described in Title IV;

4th. The service of catechesis, according to the form described in Title V, conducted according to the forms and by the persons indicated therein.

Article 2
[Implementation of the Neocatechumenal Way]
In conformity with the desire of Pope John Paul II: *"It is there-*

−*Catechism of the Catholic Church*, 1231: "By its very nature infant baptism requires a post-baptismal catechumenate. There is a need not only for instruction after baptism, but also for the necessary flowering of baptismal grace in personal growth."

−CONGREGATION FOR THE CLERGY, *General Directory for Catechesis*, 59: "The model for all catechesis is the baptismal catechumenate when, by specific formation, an adult converted to belief is brought to explicit profession of baptismal faith during the Paschal Vigil. This catechumenal formation should inspire the other forms of catechesis in both their objectives and in their dynamism." Ibid. 91: "Post-baptismal catechesis, without slavishly imitating the structure of the baptismal catechumenate and recognizing in those to be baptized the reality of their baptism, does well, however, to draw inspiration from 'this preparatory school for the Christian life,' allowing itself to be enriched by those principal elements which characterize the catechumenate."

Finally, see CONGREGATION FOR THE CLERGY, *General Directory for Catechesis*, 51: "Continuous education in the faith. In many regions this is also called 'permanent catechesis.' It is intended for those Christians who have been initiated in the basic elements of the Christian faith, but who need constantly to nourish and deepen their faith throughout their lives." Ibid, 69: "Continuing or ongoing education in the faith follows upon basic education and presupposes it. Both fulfill two distinct but complementary functions of the ministry of the Word while serving the process of continuing conversion."

[4] Cf. *Il Neocatecumenato. Un'esperienza di evangelizzazione e catechesi in atto in questa generazione. Sintesi delle sue linee di fondo*, by the Neocatechumenal Center of Rome, 1976 (*pro manuscripto*).

fore my wish that the Brothers in the Episcopate–together with their presbyters–value and help this work for the new evangelization, so that it may be implemented according to the lines proposed by the initiators, in the spirit of service to the local Ordinary and in communion with him and in the context of the unity of the local Church and the universal Church,"[5] the Neocatechumenal Way is implemented in the dioceses:

> 1st. Under the direction of the diocesan Bishop,[6] and with the guidance of the international Responsible Team of the Way, or the delegated responsible team, (cf. art. 3, §7);
>
> 2nd. According "*to the lines proposed by its initiators,*" contained in the present *Statute* and in the *Catechetical Directory of the Neocatechumenal Way,* which gather the oral tradition and the praxis of more than 30 years of the Way; this *Directory* is constituted by the text of the volumes "*Neocatechumenal Way. Guidelines for Teams of Catechists.*"

Article 3
[Competence of the international Responsible Team of the Way]

It pertains to the international Responsible Team of the Way, as indicated in Title VI:

> 1st. To make available to diocesan Bishops the spiritual goods described in art. 1 §3;
>
> 2nd. To guide the implementation of the Neocatechumenal Way and to guarantee its authenticity;
>
> 3rd. To carry out its proper tasks, as indicated in the present Statute;
>
> 4th. To proceed with those consultations which it considers appropriate;
>
> 5th. To maintain regular relations with the diocesan Bishops;
>
> 6th. To maintain regular relations with the Pontifical Council

---

[5] JOHN PAUL II, Epist. *Ogniqualvolta*, 30 August 1990, *AAS* 82 (1990) 1515.
[6] CONGREGATION FOR THE CLERGY, *General Directory for Catechesis*, 223: cf. can. 775 §1 *C.I.C.*; 617 *C.C.E.O.*

for the Laity, the dicastery to which the Holy Father has entrusted the responsibility of accompanying the Neocatechumenal Way,[7] as well as with the other dicasteries of the Holy See within the scope of their respective competence, keeping the Pontifical Council of the Laity informed;

7th. To nominate, according to the provisions of Art. 31 §2, national responsible teams – as well as, where necessary, regional and diocesan teams – delegating to them, in their respective areas, the tasks referred to in the preceding points 2, 3, 4 and 5. These teams carry out their tasks until the international Responsible Team sees fit to replace or modify them.

Article 4
[Temporal Goods]

§ 1. The Neocatechumenal Way, being an itinerary of Catholic formation that is implemented in the dioceses through services freely given, has no goods of its own.

§ 2. When in a diocese it is considered useful to support economically initiatives and activities on behalf of evangelization realized through the Neocatechumenal Way, the diocesan Bishop, at the request of the international Responsible Team of the Way, will consider the suitability of erecting an autonomous diocesan foundation, with juridical personality regulated by its own Statutes, which will also be recognized by the civil authorities. This may also be supported by donations made by participants in the Neocatechumenal Way, as well as by foundations and other individuals.

§ 3. In the community, collections may be made to answer different needs. It is the task of the responsible team of the community and of the responsible team of the Way at every level, to ensure that such collections are managed with a great sense of responsibility and respecting the law.

---

[7] Cf. JOHN PAUL II,, *Letter to Cardinal James Francis Stafford*, president, Pontifical Council for the Laity, 5 April 2001, *L'Oss. Rom.*, April 17-18, 2001, p. 4.

Title II
The Neocatechumenate or post-baptismal catechumenate

Chapter I
Fundamental Elements of the Neocatechumenate

Article 5
[Recipients]

§ 1. The Neocatechumenate is an instrument at the service of the Bishops for the rediscovery of the Christian Initiation of baptized adults. Among these, the following may be identified:[8]

1st. Those who have drifted away from the Church;

2nd. Those who have not been sufficiently evangelized and catechized;

3rd. Those who desire to deepen and mature their faith;

4th. Those who come from Christian denominations not in full communion with the Catholic Church.

§ 2. Those clerics and religious who desire to revive the gift of Baptism through the Neocatechumenate, and in this way also to serve it better, undertake it according to their vocation and their own charisms, and in fulfillment of the tasks assigned them by their diocesan Bishop or, in the case of religious, by their superior. For religious, the superior's consent is also required.[9]

Article 6
[The Neocatechumenate is implemented in the parish]

§ 1. The Neocatechumenate, being an itinerary of Christian initiation is implemented in the parish, "the usual place in which one is born and grows in the faith,"[10] the privileged location in which the Church, mother and teacher, brings to birth in the

---

[8] CONGREGATION FOR THE CLERGY, *General Directory for Catechesis*, 172.
[9] JOHN PAUL II, Ap. Ex. *Vita Consecrata*, 56.
[10] CONGREGATION FOR THE CLERGY, *General Directory for Catechesis*, 257.

baptismal font the children of God and "gestates" them to the new life.[11]

§ 2. Since the pastoral activity of Christian initiation is vital for the parish,[12] the pastor [i.e. the priest responsible for the parish, called parish priest in the UK and other countries] is at the center of the implementation of the Neocatechumenal Way,[13] exercising, together with the collaboration of other presbyters, the pastoral care of those who undertake it.[14]

§ 3. The Neocatechumenal Way will seek to foster in its recipients a mature sense of belonging to the parish, promoting a relationship of profound communion and collaboration with all the faithful and with the other elements of the parish community.

Article 7
[The Neocatechumenate implemented in small communities]

§ 1. Within the parish, the Neocatechumenate is lived in small communities – called "neocatechumenal community" – since the complete or common form for the Christian initiation of adults is communitarian.[15]

---

[11] Cf. Ibid., 79, 257; *Catechism of the Catholic Church*, 169, 507.

[12] CONGREGATION FOR THE CLERGY, *General Directory for Catechesis*, 91; cf. also 64: "Initiatory catechesis is thus the necessary link between missionary activity, which calls to faith, and pastoral activity, which continually nourishes the Christian community. This is not, therefore, an optional activity, but basic and fundamental for building up the personality of the individual disciple, as it is for the whole Christian community. Without it, missionary activity lacks continuity and is sterile, while pastoral activity lacks roots and becomes superficial and confused: any misfortune could cause the collapse of the entire building."

[13] SACRED CONGREGATION FOR DIVINE WORSHIP, *Ordo Initiationis Christianae Adultorum*, Introduction, n. 45; CONGREGATION FOR THE CLERGY, *General Directory for Catechesis*, 225.

[14] Cf. can 519 C.I.C.: "The Pastor is the proper shepherd of the parish entrusted to him, exercising pastoral care in the community entrusted to him under the authority of the diocesan Bishop in whose ministry of Christ he has been called to share;: in accord with the norm of law he carries out for his community the duties of teaching, sanctifying and governing, with the coöperation of other presbyters or deacons and the assistance of lay members of the Christian faithful;" cf. can 281 C.C.E.O.

[15] Cf. RCIA, 3; CONGREGATION FOR THE CLERGY, *General Directory for Catechesis*, 258, n. 25: "It is important to see as Pope John Paul II in *Christifideles Laici* 61

§ 2. The model of the neocatechumenal community is the *Holy Family of Nazareth*, the historical place where the Word of God, made man, becomes adult, growing "in wisdom, age and grace" and in submission to Joseph and Mary.[16] In the community the neocatechumens become adult in faith, growing in humility, simplicity and praise, and in submission to the Church.

Article 8
[Initial catecheses, neocatechumenal itinerary, "tripod" and team of catechists]

§ 1. The Neocatechumenate consists of the *initial catecheses* (Ch. II) and of the *neocatechumenal itinerary*, organized according to the three phases of Christian initiation: pre-catechumenate, catechumenate and election, divided into steps, marked by passages sealed through celebrations (Ch. IV).[17]

§ 2. The initial catecheses and the neocatechumenal itinerary are based on the three fundamental elements ("tripod") of Christian life, underlined by the Second Vatican Council: Word of God, Liturgy and Community (Ch. III).

§ 3. At the center of the whole neocatechumenal journey there is a synthesis between kerygmatic preaching, change in moral life and liturgy.[18]

---

establishes the usefulness of small ecclesial groups within the parishes and not as a parallel movement which absorbs the best members of parishes: 'Within the parishes...small ecclesial communities, where present, can be a notable help in the formation of Christians by providing a more extensive and incisive consciousness and experience of ecclesial communion and mission.'"

[16] Lk 2:52.

[17] The definitive aim of the Neocatechumenate is to put people step by step, little by little, "not only in touch, but also in communion and intimacy, with Jesus Christ" (CONGREGATION FOR THE CLERGY, *General Directory for Catechesis*, 80; cf. *RCIA*, 6), "the author and perfecter of faith." (Heb 12:2).

[18] Cf. JOHN PAUL II, *Discourse to 350 itinerant catechists of the Neocatechumenal Way*, in *L'Oss. Rom.*, 18 Jan. 1994 "Your secret is to have rediscovered a 'kerygmatic' preaching, which calls to faith also the 'far away,' realizing a postbaptismal itinerary according to the indications of the *Ordo Initiationis Christianae Adultorum* reiterated by the *Catechism of the Catholic Church* (cf. n. 1231). At the center of this journey of faith is a fruitful synthesis between preaching, change of moral life and liturgy."

§ 4. The Neocatechumenate is guided, in communion with the pastor and under his pastoral responsibility, by a team of catechists (Title V),[19] according to what is established in art. 2.

§ 5. This team, with the initial catecheses, starts a process of gestation in faith in which the communities are formed, and the team comes back periodically, usually once a year, to lead the different steps of the neocatechumenal itinerary and to give the necessary indications for the implementation of the various phases and steps.

Chapter II
The Initial Catecheses

Article 9
[Kerygma and celebrations]

The Neocatechumenate starts in the parish, at the invitation of the pastor, with kerygmatic catecheses,[20] called initial catecheses, contained in the Directory. They are given during a period of two months, in 15 evening meetings and they are concluded with a three-day *convivence*. In order to experience the Tripod–Word, Liturgy, Community–on which Christian life is based, the initial catecheses are articulated in three parts:

1st. The announcement of the kerygma which calls to conversion: the Good News of the death and resurrection of our Lord Jesus Christ;[21] "...indeed it pleased God through the folly of the kerygma to save those who believe" (1 Cor 1:21). This "word of salvation"[22] calls to conversion and to faith,[23] invites participants to recognize themselves as sinners, in order to welcome the forgiveness and gratuitous

---

[19] Congregation for the Clergy, *General Directory for Catechesis*, 156, 230-232; JOHN PAUL II, Ap. Ex. *Catechesi Tradendae*, 55; Enc. *Redemptoris Missio*, 71; can. 211 *C.I.C.*; can. 14 *C.C.E.O.*
[20] Cf. CONGREGATION FOR THE CLERGY, *General Directory for Catechesis*, 62.
[21] Cf. Rom 16:25; Acts 5:42; 8:35; 11:20. CONGREGATION FOR THE CLERGY, *General Directory for Catechesis*, 102.
[22] Acts 13:26.
[23] Cf. CONGREGATION FOR THE CLERGY, *General Directory for Catechesis*, 53-55.

love of God, and to start walking towards their personal transformation into Christ, through the power of the Spirit. Conversion is sealed by the celebration of Penance according to the rite of reconciliation of several penitents, with individual confession and absolution. This sacrament, celebrated periodically, will sustain the way of conversion of the individuals and of the community.

2nd. The kerygma prepared by God through the history of salvation (Abraham, Exodus, etc.). The hermeneutical keys, needed to listen to and understand the Sacred Scriptures, are provided: seeing in Jesus Christ the fulfillment of the Scriptures and placing the facts of one's own personal history under the light of the Word.[24] This initiation into the Scriptures is sealed with a celebration of the Word in which participants receive the Bible from the hands of the Bishop – guarantor of its authentic interpretation – as a sign that from now on along the Way mother Church will nourish them weekly at this table, living source of the catechesis.[25]

3rd. The kerygma in the sacraments and in the *koinonia*: the catecheses culminate in the convivence with the celebration of the Eucharist. This celebration, prepared by appropriate catecheses, helps rediscover the Paschal splendor emphasized by the Second Vatican Council and experience communion among the brothers and sisters. Indeed, "no Christian community is built up which does not grow from and hinge on the celebration of the most holy Eucharist. From this all education for community spirit must begin."[26] The celebration of the Eucharist will accompany the community throughout the whole itinerary.

---

[24] Cf. Ps. 119:105.
[25] JOHN PAUL II, Ap. Ex. *Catechesi Tradendæ*, 27; cf. CONGREGATION FOR THE CLERGY, *General Directory for Catechesis*, 94.
[26] VATICAN COUNCIL II, *Presbyterorum Ordinis*, 6.

Article 10
[Birth of the neocatechumenal communities]

§ 1. On the last day of the *convivence*, the Sermon on the Mount, image of the new man, is proclaimed, and the neocatechumenal itinerary is presented as a way of gestation, in the likeness of the Blessed Virgin Mary.

§ 2. Through the preaching and the celebrations done in the initial catecheses, the Holy Spirit invites men and women of different ages, mentalities, cultures and social conditions, to begin together an itinerary of conversion, based on the progressive rediscovery of the "immense and extraordinary riches and responsibilities of one's own Baptism,"[27] so as to effect in them a gradual growth and maturation in faith and in the Christian life.[28] At the end of the *convivence*, the neocatechumenal community is formed with those who welcome the call to begin this post-baptismal catechumenate.

§ 3. The neocatechumenal community is entrusted to the pastoral care of the pastor and the presbyter appointed by him (cf. Art. 27). In addition, the community, by means of a vote, chooses a lay responsible and some co-responsibles[29] who are confirmed by the pastor and the team of catechists. These collaborate with the presbyter to ensure that the community follows the itinerary of the Neocatechumenal Way according to what is established in the *Statute* and in the *Directory*, and to take care of the organizational aspects of this new community.[30]

§ 4. The team of catechists, having finished the initial catecheses, explains to the presbyter, who presides over the community, and to the team of responsibles the usual procedure of the Neocatechumenal Way for preparing the celebrations of the Word and of the Eucharist, and how to proceed with the monthly convi-

---

[27] JOHN PAUL II, Ap. Ex. *Christifideles Laici*, 61; cf. RCIA, 295.
[28] Cf. RCIA, 296.
[29] At the beginning of each step of the neocatechumenal itinerary of the Way, the responsible and the co-responsibles are confirmed by the *team of catechists*, in agreement with the pastor and presbyter of the community.
[30] Cf. PAUL VI, Ap. Ex. *Evangelii Nuntiandi*, 73.

vences, indicating the formative biblical themes for the celebration of the Word.

Chapter III
Word, Liturgy and Community

Section 1
Word of God

Article 11
[Weekly celebration of the Word]

§ 1. Every neocatechumenal community has a weekly celebration of the Word of God,[31] usually with four readings,[32] based on the themes indicated for each step by the *Catechetical Directory of the Neocatechumenal Way*.

§ 2. During the celebration of the Word of God, before the homily, the presbyter invites whoever wishes among those present to express briefly how the Word, which has just been proclaimed, has spoken to their life. In the homily, which holds a privileged place in the instruction of the Neocatechumenate,[33] the presbyter extends the proclamation of the Word,[34] interpreting it according to the Magisterium[35] and making it actual in the today of the way of faith of the neocatechumens.

§ 3. Each celebration of the Word is prepared with care, in turn, by groups of the community, with the help, whenever possi-

---

[31] This celebration follows the rite established by the *Cæremoniale Episcoporum*, n. 226.
[32] In general the first reading is taken from the *Torah* or from the historical books of the Old Testament; the second from the prophets or wisdom literature; the third from the apostolic writings and the fourth from the Gospels.
[33] Cf. *Catechism of the Catholic Church*, 132.
[34] Cf. Ibid., 1154.
[35] Cf. PONTIFICAL BIBLICAL COMMISSION, *The Interpretation of the Bible in the Church*, III, B, 3: "In so far as they are collaborators of the Bishops, the first duty of *priests* is to proclaim the Word (cf. *Presbyterorum Ordinis*, 4). They are gifted with a special charism for the interpretation of Scripture, when, transmitting not their own ideas but the Word of God, they apply the eternal truth of the gospel to the concrete circumstances of life (ibid.)."

ble, of the presbyter. The group chooses the readings[36] and the songs,[37] prepares the monitions and arranges the room and the liturgical signs for the celebration, exercising special care for its dignity and beauty.[38]

§ 4. In order to enter more deeply into the Scriptures "with the mind and the heart of the Church,"[39] the neocatechumens make use, above all, of the writings of the Fathers, of the documents of the Magisterium and, in particular, of the *Catechism of the Catholic Church*, and of the works of spiritual writers.[40]

Section 2
Liturgy

Article 12
[Paschal Vigil]

§ 1. The summit and source of Christian life is the paschal mystery, lived and celebrated in a preëminent way in the Sacred Triduum,[41] whose brilliance fills with light the whole liturgical year.[42] For this reason, it constitutes the fulcrum of the Neocatechumenate, since it is a rediscovering of Christian initiation.

§ 2. "The Paschal Vigil, focal point of the Christian liturgy, and its baptismal spirituality inspire all Catechesis."[43] It is for this

---

[36] To this end, the neocatechumens make use of tools like the *Dictionary of Biblical Theology* of X. LEON-DUFOUR or the parallel texts and notes of the *Jerusalem Bible*, etc.

[37] In the Neocatechumenal Way a book is used of songs taken from the Word of God and from the Christian and Jewish liturgical tradition, which progressively emphasize the contents of the various steps and passages.

[38] Cf. *Institutio Generalis Missalis Romani*, 253.

[39] JOHN PAUL II, Ap. Ex. *Catechesi Tradendæ*, 27; cf. CONGREGATION FOR THE CLERGY, *General Directory for Catechesis*, 127.

[40] CONGREGATION FOR THE CLERGY, *General Directory for Catechesis*, 128,96.

[41] Cf. *Roman Missal, Announcement of the Day of Easter on the Solemnity of the Epiphany:* "The center of the whole liturgical year is the Triduum of the Lord's crucifixion, burial and resurrection."

[42] Cf. *Catechism of the Catholic Church*, 1168.

[43] Congregation for the Clergy, *General Directory for Catechesis*, 91; cf. "The baptismal catechumenate is wholly penetrated by Christ's paschal mystery. Therefore 'all of initiation has to clearly reveal its paschal character'" (RCIA, 8); cf. Ibid., 59.

reason that during the itinerary, the neocatechumens are initiated gradually[44] into an ever more perfect participation in all that the holy night signifies, celebrates and fulfills.

§ 3. In this way, the Neocatechumenate contributes to forming little by little a parish assembly which prepares and celebrates the Paschal Vigil on the holy night, with all the richness of the liturgical and sacramental features and the signs asked for by the Church.[45]

Article 13
[Eucharist]

§ 1. The Eucharist is essential to the Neocatechumenate since the Neocatechumenate is a post-baptismal catechumenate, lived in small communities.[46] Indeed, the Eucharist completes Christian initiation.[47]

§ 2. The neocatechumens celebrate the Eucharist in the small community in order to be gradually initiated into full, conscious and active participation in the divine mysteries,[48] according to the

---

[44] Even today, many neocatechumens come from the world and experiences outside of the church and they need a gradual introduction to the sacraments: a sacramental pedagogy that John Paul II has defined as a "sacramental laboratory," in which the baptized, but not initiated, may gradually discover the splendor of the paschal mystery (cf. KAROL WOJTYLA, *Affinche Cristo si serva di noi. Catecumenato del XX Secolo* Krakow: Znak, 34, 1952, pp. 402-413).

[45] CONGREGATION FOR THE DIVINE WORSHIP, litt. circ. *Paschalis sollemnitatis*, 39-42, 77-96.

[46] JOHN PAUL II, letter *Ogniquavolta*, 30 Aug 1990: *AAS* 82 (1990) 1515: "It is the announcement of the Gospel, the testimony in small communities and the celebration of the Eucharist in groups (cf. "Notification on celebrations in groups of the Neocatechumenal Way," *L'Oss. Rom.*, 24 Dec 1988) which empower the members to place themselves at the service of the Church's renewal;" (IDEM., "Discourse to 350 itinerant catechists of the Neocatechumenal Way," in *L'Oss. Rom.*, 18 Jan 1994; "All of this is actuated in small communities in which 'reflection on the Word of God and participation in the Eucharist…form living cells in the church, renew the vitality of the parish through mature Christians capable of witnessing to the truth with a faith which is radically lived" (Message to the Bishops of Europe gathered in Vienna, 12 April 1993).

[47] Cf. *RCIA*, 36, 368.

[48] Cf. ibid., *Sacrosanctum Concilium*, 48; CONGREGATION FOR THE CLERGY, *General Directory for Catechesis*, 85; St. LEO THE GREAT, *Sermo 12, De passione*: "Our participation in the body and blood of Christ does no less than transform

example of Christ who, in the multiplication of loaves, made the people sit down "in groups of 50" (Lk 9:14). This custom, consolidated in the more than 30-year-old praxis of the Way, has born rich fruit.[49]

§ 3. In consideration also "of specific formative and pastoral needs, taking account of the good of individuals or groups, and especially of the fruits which may be derived from them for the entire Christian community,"[50] the small neocatechumenal community,[51] with the authorization of the diocesan Bishop, celebrates the dominical Eucharist after first vespers,[52] open also to other faithful.

§ 4. Each celebration of the Eucharist is prepared, when possible under the guidance of the presbyter, by a group of the neocate-

---

us into what we receive, to be clothed completely, in body and in spirit, in him in whom we have died, been buried and are raised."

[49] In this way the needs of contemporary man are met: Sunday is given a special value, avoiding the dispersion which is part of the weekend, young people are rescued from Saturday evening discos and drugs, the family is given the possibility of being united in a domestic liturgy—a privileged moment in the transmission of the faith to children—and brothers and sisters who are more advanced in their formation are given the opportunity to animate the Sunday Masses of the parish; but above all, the intensity of participation in the small community stimulate and provokes a moral change, promoting numerous vocations to the priesthood and religious and missionary life.

[50] JOHN PAUL II, apos. letter *Dies Domini*, 36: cf. SACRED CONGREGATION FOR DIVINE WORSHIP, *Instructio Actio Pastoralis de Missis pro coetibus particularibus*: "The pastors of souls are exhorted strongly to consider favorably and deepen the spiritual and formative value of these celebrations."

[51] Cf. JOHN PAUL II, *Discourse to 350 itinerant catechists of the Neocatechumenal Way*, in *L'Oss. Rom.*, 18 Jan 1994: "Your experience of many years now in the 'Way' will certainly have taught you that the small community, sustained by the Word of God and the dominical Eucharist, becomes a place of communion."

[52] Cf. *Notification of the Congregation for Divine Worship on the Celebrations of the Groups of the Neocatechumenal Way* in *L'Oss. Rom.*, Dec 24, 1988: "The Congregation consents that among the adaptations foreseen by the Instruction 'Actio Pastoralis,' n. 6-11, the groups of the above-mentioned 'Way' may receive communion under two species, always with unleavened bread and transfer *ad experimentum* the Rite of Peace to after the Prayer of the Faithful." Following what is said in the Instruction *Ecclesia de mysterio* (art. 3, § 3), to prepare the assembly to better welcome the homily, the presbyter, with prudence, can give the possibility to some among those who are present to briefly express what the proclaimed Word has said to their life.

chumenal community, in turn, which prepares brief monitions to the readings, chooses the songs, provides the bread, the wine, the flowers, and takes care of the decorum and dignity of the liturgical signs.

Article 14
[Penance, prayer, the liturgical year, devotional practices]

§ 1. "The sacrament of penance contributes in a preëminent way to sustain Christian life."[53] In their itinerary of conversion, the neocatechumens celebrate it periodically according to the rite of reconciliation for several penitents with individual confession and absolution. Beyond this, they are introduced to a regular use of the sacrament of Penance according to the rite of reconciliation for a single penitent.

§ 2. The neocatechumens are gradually initiated into liturgical and private prayer.[54] Parents are instructed on how to transmit the faith to their children[55] in a domestic celebration during Sunday Lauds.[56] The children are prepared for their First Communion and for Confirmation in the parish and after their thirteenth year are invited to begin the Neocatechumenal Way.

§ 3. The Church progressively initiates the neocatechumens to the catechetical and spiritual riches of the liturgical year, in which she "celebrates the complete mystery of Christ."[57] To this end, the catechists give a preparatory announcement before Advent, Lent and Easter.

§ 4. The neocatechumens are also instructed gradually in Eucharistic devotion outside Mass, in nocturnal adoration, in the recitation of the holy Rosary and in other traditional Catholic practices of piety.

---

[53] SECOND VATICAN COUNCIL, *Christus Dominus*, 30, cf. can. 718-736, C.C.E.O.
[54] Cf. art. 20, 1° and 3°.
[55] Cf. CONGREGATION FOR THE CLERGY, *General Directory for Catechesis*, 226-227, 255; Can. 774 § 2 C.I.C., 618 C.C.E.O.
[56] Cf. *Institutio Generalis Liturgiae Horarum*, 27.
[57] *Normae Universalis de Anno Liturgico et de Calendario*, 17; cf. can. 619, C.C.E.O.

Section 3
Community

Article 15
[The communitarian aspect and "convivence"]

§ 1. Education in community life is one of the fundamental tasks of Christian initiation.[58] The Neocatechumenate nurtures people in community life in a gradual and constant way by inserting them into a small community, as the body of the risen Christ, open to the life of the parish community and of the whole Church.

§ 2. A special moment for this education is the monthly day of *convivence* for every neocatechumenal community. In the *convivence*, after the celebration of Lauds, people share freely the experience of what God's grace is accomplishing in their life and the difficulties which may have occurred are expressed, respecting the freedom of a person's conscience. This fosters knowledge and reciprocal enlightenment and mutual encouragement in seeing God's action in the history of everyone.

§ 3. The community helps the neocatechumens to discover their need for conversion and maturation in faith: differences, defects and weaknesses show clearly the incapacity to love one another as they are, thus destroying false ideals of community and providing the experience that communion (*koinonia*) is the work of the Holy Spirit.[59]

Article 16
[The experience of koinonia *and the fruits of the community]*

§ 1. As the neocatechumens grow in faith, signs of *koinonia* begin to appear: not judging, not resisting evil, forgiving and loving the enemy.[60] *Koinonia* is also made visible in helping the needy, caring for the sick, the suffering and the old, and in providing, as far as possible, for those who are in mission, according to

---

[58] Cf. CONGREGATION FOR THE CLERGY, *General Directory for Catechesis*, 86.
[59] Cf. ibid., 253: "The Christian community is the historical realization of the gift of 'communion' (*koinonia*), which is a fruit of the Holy Spirit."
[60] Cf. Lk 6:27-37; Mt 5: 38-48.

the guidelines of the *Directory*. The neocatechumens are gradually formed in an ever more profound spirit of communion and reciprocal help.

§ 2. The Neocatechumenate thus progressively forms in the parish an ensemble of communities which make visible the signs of love in the dimension of the Cross[61] and of perfect unity.[62] In this way they call to faith the far away and prepare non-Christians to receive the announcement of the Gospel.

§ 3. The Neocatechumenal Way is thus offered as an apt instrument to help the parish fulfill more and more the ecclesial mission to be salt, light and leaven of the world,[63] and to shine before men as the visible Body of the risen Jesus Christ,[64] universal sacrament of salvation.[65]

Article 17
[Initiation to mission]

§ 1. "Catechesis prepares the Christian to live in community and to participate actively in the life and mission of the Church."[66] The neocatechumens are initiated to "be present as Christians in society"[67] and "to lend their coöperation to the different ecclesial services, according to their proper vocation."[68]

§ 2. The neocatechumens collaborate "actively in the evangelization and edification of the Church,"[69] above all by being what they are:[70] their decision to live the Christian vocation in an

---

[61] Cf. Jn 13:34-35: "A new commandment I give to you, that you love one another. By this everyone will know that you are my disciples."
[62] Cf. Jn 17:21: "Even as you, Father, are in me, and I in you, that they also may be in us, so that the world may believe that you have sent me."
[63] Cf. Mt 5:13-16; 13:33.
[64] Cf. SECOND VATICAN COUNCIL, *Lumen Gentium*, 7-8.
[65] Cf. ibid., 48; SECOND VATICAN COUNCIL, *Gaudium et Spes*, 45.
[66] Congregation for the Clergy, *General Directory for Catechesis*, 86.
[67] Ibid.
[68] Ibid.; cf. can. 210 *c.i.c.*, 13 *C.C.E.O.*
[69] *RCIA*, 19, 4.
[70] Cf. PAUL VI, *General Audience*, 8 May 1974, *Notitiae*, 95-96, 230: "This purpose, while it is for you an authentic way of living the Christian vocation, becomes an effective testimony for others—you make apostolate *just because you*

authentic way becomes an effective witness for others, as well as a stimulus for rediscovering Christian values which might otherwise remain almost hidden.

§ 3 After a suitable period of time in the Way,[71] each neocatechumenal community chooses by vote some brothers and sisters to undertake the task of catechists. These, if they accept this designation, having been previously approved by the pastor and by the catechists who guide the community, constitute, together with the presbyter and with the responsible of the community, a team of catechists, to evangelize and guide new communities, either in their own or another parish, or in another diocese[72] at the request of the respective pastors or diocesan ordinaries.

§ 4. The neocatechumens collaborate in the missionary and pastoral work of the parish and of the diocese. Before the "*Redditio symboli*,[73] considering the maturity of their faith, those who so wish can offer their help; after the *Redditio*, as an integral part of Christian initiation, the neocatechumens take part in various ecclesial services, according to each one's own vocation.

Article 18
[Initiation to and formation in the priestly vocation]

§ 1. The Neocatechumenal Way, as very true itinerary of catechesis, is also a "means to foster vocations to the priesthood, and of particular consecration to God in the different forms of religious and apostolic life and to enkindle in the heart of individuals their special missionary vocation."[74]

§ 2. The Neocatechumenal Way is also an instrument that is offered at the service of the Bishops for the Christian formation of candidates to the presbyterate.

---

are what you are—in a stimulus for the rediscovery and recovery of true, authentic, effective Christian values, which might otherwise remain almost hidden, dulled and quite watered down in everyday life."

[71] Usually after the second scrutiny of passage to the post-baptismal catechumenate.
[72] CONGREGATION FOR THE CLERGY, *General Directory for Catechesis*, 268.
[73] Cf. art. 20, 2°.
[74] CONGREGATION FOR THE CLERGY, *General Directory for Catechesis*, 86.

§ 3. The diocesan missionary "Redemptoris Mater" Seminaries are erected by the diocesan Bishops, in agreement with the international Responsible Team of the Way and are governed by the current norms for the formation and incardination of diocesan clerics[75] and according to their own Statutes, in fulfillment of the *Ratio fundamentalis institutionis sacerdotalis*.[76] In them the candidates for the priesthood find in participation in the Neocatechumenal Way, a specific and basic element of their formative itinerary and, at the same time, are prepared for a "genuine presbyteral choice of service to the entire people of God in the fraternal communion of the presbyterate."[77]

§ 4. It is the task of the diocesan Bishop to appoint, upon presentation by the international Responsible Team of the Way, the rector and the other superiors and educators of the "Redemptoris Mater" diocesan missionary seminaries. The rector, in the name of the Bishop and in close coöperation with him, oversees the studies of the seminarians and their formative itinerary, and discerns the suitability of candidates for the priesthood.

Chapter IV
The Neocatechumenal itinerary: phases, steps and passages

Article 19
[1ˢᵗ phase: post-baptismal precatechumenate]

§ 1. The first phase of the neocatechumenate is the *post-baptismal precatechumenate* which is a time of *kenosis*[78] in order to learn to walk in *humility*.[79] It is divided into two steps:

1ˢᵗ. In the first step, which goes from the initial catecheses until the first scrutiny of passage to the post-baptismal catechumenate, and which lasts approximately two years,

---

[75] Cf. cann. 232-272 C.I.C. and 331-366 C.C.E.O.
[76] CONGREGATION FOR CATHOLIC EDUCATION, *Ratio Fundamentalis Institutionis Sacerdotalis*, Mar 19, 1985, n. 94-99.
[77] JOHN PAUL II, Ap. Ex. *Pastores dabo vobis*, n. 68.
[78] Cf. Phil 2:7.
[79] Cf. Mic 6:8.

the neocatechumens learn the language of the Bible by celebrating each week the Word of God, with simple themes that take them throughout the whole of Scripture, like water, rock, lamb, etc. The *Word of God*, the *Eucharist* and the *community* gradually help the neocatechumens to be emptied of false concepts of themselves and of God and to descend into their reality of sinners in need of conversion, rediscovering the gratuity of the love of Christ, who forgives them and loves them.

In the concluding celebration of the *first scrutiny* of passage to the post-baptismal catechumenate, after the inscription of the name, they ask the Church to help them mature in the faith in order to do works of eternal life,[80] and then they receive the sign of the glorious Cross of Christ, which illuminates the salvific role of the Cross in the life of each one.

2nd. In the second step, of similar length, the neocatechumens celebrate the great phases of the history of salvation: Abraham, Exodus, Desert, Promised Land, etc., and a time is given to them so that they may prove to themselves the sincerity of their intention to follow Jesus Christ[81] in the light of his Word: "You cannot serve both God and money" (Mt 6:24).

In the concluding rite of the *second scrutiny* of passage to the post-baptismal catechumenate, they renew before the Church the renunciation of the devil and they manifest the will to serve God alone. Thereafter, they study and celebrate the main biblical figures: Adam, Eve, Cain, Abel, Noah, etc. in the light of Christ.

§ 2. The scrutinies help the neocatechumens in their way of conversion, respecting the conscience and the internal forum, ac-

---

[80] Cf. 1 Jn 3:14-15; Eph 2:10: "For we are his workmanship, created in Christ Jesus for good works, which God prepared beforehand, that we should walk in them."
[81] Cf. Lk 14:25-33.

cording to the canonical norms,[82] the RCIA and the *Catechetical Directory of the Neocatechumenal Way*.

Article 20
[2nd phase: post-baptismal catechumenate]

The second phase of the Neocatechumenate is the *post-baptismal catechumenate* which is a time[83] of spiritual battle to acquire the interior *simplicity* of the new man who loves God as the only Lord, with all his heart, with all his mind, with all his strength, and his neighbor as himself.[84] Sustained by the Word of God, by the Eucharist and by the community, the neocatechumens are trained in the fight against the temptations of the devil: the search for securities, the scandal of the Cross and the seduction of the idols of the world.[85] The Church comes to the aid of the neocatechumens giving them the necessary weapons in three steps:

> 1st. "The spiritual battle of the Christian's new life is inseparable from the battle of prayer,"[86] which leads to intimacy with God. The Church carries out a first initiation of the neocatechumens into liturgical and personal prayer, as well as nocturnal prayer,[87] which culminates with the catechesis of the Gospels on prayer and the celebration of the *handing over* of the book of the *Liturgy of the Hours*. Henceforth, they begin each day with the personal prayer of Lauds and of the Office of Readings and they learn to have a time for silent prayer and for the prayer of the heart.
>
> The neocatechumens scrutinizing the Psalms in small groups, are initiated into the assiduous practice of the *lect-*

---

[82] Cf. Canons 220 C.I.C. and 23 C.C.E.O.
[83] Cf. R.C.I.A. 20: "The length of time of the catechumenate depends on the grace of God and on different circumstances. Therefore nothing can be established *a priori.*"
[84] Cf. Mk 12:30-31; Dt 6:4-5.
[85] Cf. Mt 4:1-11.
[86] *Catechism of the Catholic Church*, 2725; cf. CONGREGATION FOR THE EASTERN CHURCHES, Instruction for the application of the liturgical prescription from the Code of Canons of the Eastern Churches (6-1-19960) n. 95-9.
[87] Cf. *Institutio Generalis de Liturgia Horarum*, 10, 57-58, 72.

io divina or *scrutatio scripturae*[88] "in which the Word of God is read and meditated upon to be transformed into prayer."[89] Indeed, "ignorance of the Scriptures is ignorance of Christ."[90]

2nd. The Church hands over to the neocatechumens the Creed (*Traditio Symboli*), "the compendium of Scripture and faith,"[91] and sends them to preach it, two by two, to the homes of the parish. They study and celebrate the Apostles' Creed article by article and then give it back to the Church (*Redditio Symboli*), confessing their faith and proclaiming the Creed solemnly before the faithful, during Lent.

3rd. The Church begins a second initiation of the neocatechumens into liturgical and contemplative prayer, which culminates with the catecheses on the Lord's Prayer and with the rite of the *handing over of the "Our Father,"* "summary of the whole Gospel."[92] Henceforth, on the weekdays of Advent and Lent, they begin to celebrate as a community in the parish, before going to work, Lauds and the Office of Readings, with a time of contemplative prayer.

The neocatechumens are initiated to become "little ones"[93] and to live in filial abandonment to the fatherhood of God, protected by the maternity of Mary and the Church, and in fidelity to the successor of Peter and to the Bishop. For this reason, before the handing over of the "Our Father," the neocatechumens make a pilgrimage to a Marian shrine to welcome the Virgin Mary as mother[94] and they profess their faith upon the tomb of

---

[88] Cf. Jn 5:39.
[89] *Catechism of the Catholic Church*, 1177; cf. PONTIFICAL BIBLICAL COMMISSION, *The Interpretation of the Bible in the Church*, IV, C, 2.
[90] SAINT JEROME, *Comm. in Is.*, Prol; cf. SECOND ECUMENICAL VATICAN COUNCIL, *Dei Verbum*, 25; *Catechism of the Catholic Church*, 133.
[91] CONGREGATION FOR THE CLERGY, *General Directory for Catechesis*, 85.
[92] Ibid.; *Catechism of the Catholic Church*, 2761.
[93] Cf. Mt 18:4.
[94] Cf. Jn 19:26-27.

Saint Peter and make an act of adherence to the Pope.

In this step, the neocatechumens study in a systematic way the individual petitions of the "Our Father" plus themes on the Virgin Mary: Mother of the Church, New Eve, Ark of the Covenant, Image of the Christian, etc.

Article 21
[3rd phase: rediscovering election]

§ 1. The third phase of the Neocatechumenate is the rediscovery of the election, "summit of the entire catechumenate."[95] During this time of enlightenment, the Church teaches the neocatechumens to walk in *praise*, "flooded by the light of faith,"[96] discerning and fulfilling God's will in history by making their own lives a *liturgy of holiness*. They study and celebrate the individual passages of the Sermon on the Mount.

§ 2. Having shown with their works that the new man described in the Sermon on the Mount is becoming a reality in them even in their weakness – the new man who, following the footsteps of Jesus Christ,[97] does not resist evil and loves the enemy,[98] the neocatechumens *solemnly renew their baptismal promises in the Paschal Vigil* presided over by the Bishop. In this liturgy, they wear white garments as a reminder of their Baptism.

§ 3. Then, during the 50 days of Eastertide, they solemnly celebrate the Eucharist every day and make a pilgrimage to the Holy Land as a sign of their wedding feast with the Lord, visiting the places where Christ fulfilled all that they have lived throughout the neocatechumenal itinerary.

§ 4. After the election, the post-baptismal Neocatechumenate ends.

---

[95] *RCIA*, 23.
[96] Ibid., 24.
[97] Cf. 1 Pt 2:21
[98] Cf. Mt 5:39-45.

Title III
Ongoing education in the faith: a way of renewal in the parish

Article 22
[Ongoing education in the small community]

§ 1. The Neocatechumenal Community, after having completed the itinerary of rediscovery of Christian initiation, enters into the process of ongoing education in the faith: continuing the weekly celebration of the Word and the dominical Eucharist and in fraternal communion, actively involved into the pastoral work of the parish community, in order to give signs of love[99] and unity,[100] which call contemporary man to faith.

"Ongoing formation in the faith – as the *General Directory for Catechesis* affirms – is directed not only to Christians individually to accompany them on their journey towards holiness, but also to the Christian community as such so that it may mature also in its interior life of love of God and of the brethren, as well as in its openness to the world as missionary community. The desire of Jesus and his prayer to the Father are an unceasing appeal: 'May they all be one; even as You, Father, are in me, and I in You, that they may also be in us, so that the world may believe that You have sent me' (Jn 17:21). Approaching this ideal, little by little, demands of the *community* a great faithfulness to the Holy Spirit's action, the constant nourishment of the *Body and Blood of the Lord* and ongoing education in the faith by listening to the *Word.*"[101]

§ 2. The Neocatechumenal Way is thus an instrument at the service of the Bishops to implement the process of ongoing education in the faith required by the Church: Christian initiation, as underlined by the *General Directory for Catechesis*, "is not the final point in the process of continuing conversion. The profession of

---

[99] Cf. Jn 13:34-35: "A new commandment I give to you, that you love one another. By this everyone will know that you are my disciples."
[100] Cf. Jn 17:21: "Even as you, Father, are in me, and I in you, that they also may be in us, so that the world may believe that you have sent me."
[101] CONGREGATION FOR THE CLERGY, *General Directory for Catechesis,* 70 (italics added).

baptismal faith is the foundation of a spiritual building which is destined to grow,"[102] so "adhering to Jesus Christ, in fact, sets in motion a process of ongoing conversion, which lasts for the whole of life."[103]

Article 23
[A way of renewal in the parish]

§ 1. Thus, the Neocatechumenal Way contributes to the parish renewal hoped for by the Magisterium of the Church: to foster "new methods and structures," which avoid anonymity and massive numbers[104] and to consider "the parish as a community of communities,"[105] which makes "the parish community decentralized and articulated."[106]

§ 2. The team of catechists who guided the community during the neocatechumenal itinerary, in a way analogous to that of the godparents for Baptism,[107] remains available for the necessities of the evangelization and ongoing formation.

---

[102] Ibid., 56.
[103] Ibid.; cf. also 69-72.
[104] Cf. JOHN PAUL II, "Discourse to the Conference of Catholic Bishops of Ontario," *L'Oss. Rom.*, 5 May 1999: *"We cannot allow the anonymity of the cities to invade our Eucharist communities.* We need to find new methods and new structures to build bridges between people, in such a way that there is truly realized that experience of reciprocal acceptance and closeness demanded of Christian fraternity. It may be that this experience and the catechesis which must accompany it is realized in smaller communities, as is specified in the Post-Synodal Exhortation: 'One way of renewing parishes, which is especially urgent in the parishes of the large cities, may perhaps be found in considering the parish as a community of communities'" *(Ecclesia in America*, n. 41). John Paul II, *Alla Parrocchia di Santa Maria Goretti*, 31 Jan 1988, *L'Oss. Rom.* 1-2 Feb 1988: "There is a way, I think, to rebuild the parish based on the neocatechumenal experience...this is very coherent with the very nature of the parish." Also his *Message to the Bishops of Europe* gathered in Vienna, 12 April 1993: "[Such communities] form living cells of the church, renew the vitality of the parish through mature Christians capable of witnessing to the truth with a faith radically lived."
[105] JOHN PAUL II, Ap. Ex. *Ecclesia in America*, n. 41: "One way of renewing parishes, which is especially urgent in parishes of large cities, may perhaps be found in considering the parish as a community of communities."
[106] JOHN PAUL II, ap. ex. *Redemptoris Missio*, 51.
[107] Cf. can. 872, 892; 684, 685 *C.C.E.O.*

Title IV
Baptismal Catechumenate
Article 24
[Catechumens]

§ 1. The Neocatechumenal Way is also an instrument at the service of the Bishop for the Christian initiation of the non-baptized.

§ 2. The participation in the initial catecheses and in the first phase of the neocatechumenal itinerary – according to their proper status – of those who must follow the catechumenate according to the norm of law[108] guarantees that all that is required by the RCIA will be adequately implemented. In particular:

> 1st. The Christian initiation of the catechumens "takes place step by step in the midst of the community of the faithful. Together with the catechumens, the faithful reflect upon the value of the paschal mystery, renew their own conversion, and by their example lead the catechumens to obey the Holy Spirit more generously."[109]
>
> 2nd. "The people of God, represented by the local Church, should always understand and show that the initiation of adults is their concern and the business of all the baptized. ... Each disciple of Christ ... must help the candidates and catechumens throughout the whole period of initiation, during the pre-catechumenate, the catechumenate, and the period of post-baptismal catechesis or mystagogia."[110]
>
> 3rd. "That time of evangelization, in which faith and initial conversion take their origin, should not be omitted,..." nor "the period of the pre-catechumenate" required "so that the true desire of following Christ and seeking Bap-

---

[108] Cf. *Code of Canon Law*, 206, 788, 852 § 1, 865 § 1, 1183 § 1; 9, 30, 587-588 C.C.E.O.
[109] *RCIA*, n. 4. of the *editio typica* corresponds to n. 4 of 1990, ICEL.
[110] Ibid., n. 41. of the *editio typica* corresponds to n. 9 of 1990, ICEL.

tism may mature."[111]

4th. Before admission to the catechumenate, it is necessary that the candidates "have begun to have a sense of repentance, to invoke God and pray to Him, to have a first experience of community and of Christian spirituality."[112]

5th. "The catechumens, who have been welcomed by the Church with a mother's love and with her care as already her children, are joined to her, belong to the family of Christ: indeed they receive from the Church the nourishment of the word of God and are sustained with the help of the liturgy."[113] Thus "celebrations of the Word of God are arranged for their benefit, and at Mass they may also attend the liturgy of the Word with the faithful, better preparing themselves for participation in the Eucharist in time to come."[114]

6th. "When they are present in the assembly of the faithful, they should be dismissed in a friendly manner before the Eucharistic celebration begins."[115] In the Neocatechumenal Way this is done through a special blessing,[116] after which they receive "a fitting catechesis" prepared on the basis of the *Catechism of the Catholic Church* which "leads the catechumens to a suitable knowledge of dogma and precepts and also to an intimate understanding of the mystery of salvation."[117]

7th. "The catechumens also learn to collaborate actively in evangelization and in building up the Church."[118]

---

[111] Ibid., n. 9-11 of the *editio typica* corresponds to n. 36 of 1990, ICEL.
[112] Ibid., n. 15 of the *editio typica* corresponds to n. 42 of 1990, ICEL.
[113] Ibid., n. 18 of the *editio typica* corresponds to n. 47 of 1990, ICEL; cf. *Code of Canon Law*, 206; 9 C.C.E.O.
[114] RCIA, n. 19,3 of the *editio typica* corresponds to n. 75,3 of 1990, ICEL.
[115] Ibid., corresponds to n. 75,3 of 1990, ICEL.
[116] Cf. Ibid., n. 119-124 of the *editio typica* corresponds to n. 116 of 1990, ICEL.
[117] Ibid., n. 19,1 of the *editio typica* corresponds to n. 75,1 of 1990, ICEL.
[118] Ibid., n. 19,4. of the *editio typica* corresponds to n. 75,4 of 1990, ICEL.

§ 3. To complete the preparation for Baptism and celebrate this in the Paschal Vigil, it is normally appropriate for them to wait for the conclusion of the second scrutiny, after about four years. This decision is to be taken by the pastor together with the team of catechists.

Article 25
[Neophytes]

§ 1. Having completed the period of preparation, in agreement with the pastor and with appropriate communication to the diocesan Bishop,[119] the catechumens receive the sacraments of Christian initiation[120] (Baptism, confirmation, Eucharist) and are thus fully incorporated into the Church.

§ 2. Those who wish will continue to participate in the life of the neocatechumenal community with which they have walked until then as catechumens, and they will proceed with the two other phases of the neocatechumenal itinerary: "The community and the neophytes continue on the Way meditating the Gospel, sharing in the Eucharist and performing works of charity. In this way they understand the paschal mystery more fully and bring into their lives more and more."[121] This provides a precious help for the neophytes to overcome the difficulties intrinsic to the first years of Christian life.

Title V
Form of service to the catechesis

Article 26
[Diocesan Bishop]

It pertains to the diocesan Bishop, as responsible for Christian initiation, formation and life in the local Church:[122]

1st. To authorize the implementation of the Neocatechumenal

---

[119] Cf. can. 863, *C.I.C.*
[120] Cf. can. 866, *C.I.C.;* 695, 697 *C.C.E.O.*
[121] *RCIA*, n. 37 of the *editio typica* corresponds to n. 244 of 1990, ICEL.
[122] Cf. CONGREGATION FOR THE CLERGY, *General Directory for Catechesis*, 222-223; *RCIA*, general intro. 12; intro. 44, 66.

Way in the diocese;

2nd. To watch over the implementation of the Neocatechumenal Way so that it may take place in conformity with what is established in art. 1 and 2, respecting the doctrine and the discipline of the Church;

3rd. To provide for a reasonable pastoral continuity in the parishes where the Neocatechumenal Way is present;

4th. To preside personally or through a delegate, over the rites which mark the passages of the Neocatechumenal itinerary;

5th. To resolve, in dialogue with the Responsible Team of the Way, according to Art. 3, questions which may arise with regard to the implementation and the development of the Way in his diocese;

6th. To ensure a productive collaboration between the diocesan neocatechumenal center, according to art. 30, and the various offices of the diocesan Curia (in particular the liturgical and catechetical offices).

Article 27
[Pastor and presbyters]

§ 1. The pastor and the presbyters carry out the pastoral care of those who follow the Neocatechumenal Way – in keeping with Art. 5 §2 and 6 §2 – and fulfill *"in persona Christi capitis"* the priestly ministry announcing the Word of God, administering the sacraments and, as far as possible, presiding over the celebrations of the first or of other neocatechumenal communities in the parish.

§ 2. In addition, the pastor and the presbyters:

1st. In the name of the diocesan Bishop watch over the implementation of the Way so that it may take place in conformity with Art. 1 and 2, in respect of the doctrine and of the discipline of the Church;

2nd. Help the teams of catechists, in accordance with Art. 8 §4 and §5, to carry out their mission;

3rd. Given that the pastoral work of Christian initiation is vital for evangelizing contemporary man, support the implementation of the Way as one of the pastoral instruments of the parish.

Article 28
[Catechists]

§ 1. The teams of catechists are composed of some lay faithful, elected in conformity with Art. 17 §3, and a presbyter.

§ 2. The teams of catechists, as expressed in this *Statute*[123] and in the *Catechetical Directory of the Neocatechumenal Way*,

1st. Upon the invitation of the pastor, give the initial catecheses which begin a process of gestation to faith through which the communities are formed;

2nd. Return periodically, usually once a year, to conduct the various passages of the neocatechumenal itinerary and give the necessary guidance for continuing the various phases and steps;

3rd. Exercise an important role of discernment as to the readiness of individual catechumens and their respective communities with regard to the passage to the various stages of the itinerary of the Way;

4th. During the scrutinies of the passage guided by them, they are to maintain the maximum respect for the moral aspects of the private life of the neocatechumens which belong to the internal forum of the person.

§ 3. In exercising their task, the lay catechists collaborate with the pastor and with the presbyters of the respective communities and help in their mission of the governing, of teaching and of sanctification which is proper to them as ordained ministers.

---

[123] Cf. art. 17 § 3 and 31.

Article 29
[Formation of Catechists]

In order for catechists to acquire – as required by the *General Directory for Catechesis* – "the evangelical attitudes which Jesus taught his disciples when he sent them on mission:…to seek out the lost sheep, proclaim and heal at the same time, to be poor, without money or knapsack; to know how to accept rejection and persecution; to place one's trust in the Father and in the support of the Holy Spirit; to expect no other reward than the joy of working for the Kingdom,"[124] they are suitably prepared:

1st. The basis of their formation is participation in the Neocatechumenate which guarantees their gradual growth in faith and in witness[125] with a corresponding deepening of their biblical, patristic and theological formation, with particular reference to the documents of the Magisterium of the Church;

2nd. They prepare themselves to transmit the Word as they in their turn have received[126] and lived it: they are trained by accompanying several times their own catechists during the initial catecheses and the various passages of the Neocatechumenate;

3rd. They complete their formation by participating in appropriate *convivences* and meetings of catechists called by the international Responsible Team of the Way or by a team delegated by them in which fundamental themes of the church's Magisterium are addressed;

4th. They participate in the meetings held in the *Diocesan Neocatechumenal Center*, as described in the following article, for the formation of catechists;

---

[124] Cf. CONGREGATION FOR THE CLERGY, *General Directory for Catechesis*, 86; cf. Mt 1:5-42; Lk 10:1-20.

[125] CONGREGATION FOR THE CLERGY, *General Directory for Catechesis*, 246-247: "When the faith of the catechists is not yet mature, it is advisable that they participate in an itinerary of a catechumenal type."

[126] Cf. 1 Cor 15:1-11; CONGREGATION FOR THE CLERGY, *General Directory for Catechesis*, 235-236.

5th. Finally, they prepare each catechesis and passage of the Neocatechumenate, together with the presbyter in so far as it is possible, reading in an atmosphere of prayer the corresponding passages of Sacred Scripture, the *Catechism of the Catholic Church* and of the *Catechetical Directory of the Neocatechumenal Way* which revive in them the "word of salvation" (Acts 13:26) which they themselves received orally from their own catechists.

Article 30
[Neocatechumenal center]

§ 1. Whenever the development of the Neocatechumenal Way in a diocese requires it, the team of catechists which opened the Way sets up and guides, in agreement with the Bishop, a center called the *Diocesan Neocatechumenal Center* to promote meetings between the Bishop or his delegate, the pastors, and the presbyters, catechists and responsibles of the communities.

§ 2. The scope of the center is to contribute to the formation of the catechists, to assign the new catecheses, to coördinate the various passages and to support the teams of catechists in the various difficulties of evangelization and to present to the Bishop or to his delegate the responsibles of the new communities.

Article 31
[Itinerant catechists]

§ 1. In the *convivences* of catechists, described in Art. 29, 3rd, to answer the requests of distant dioceses, a call is made to the participants to make themselves available to be sent as *itinerants* to any part of the world. Those who feel called by God indicate their availability.

§ 2. In appropriate *convivences*, the international Responsible Team of the Way constitutes *teams of itinerant catechists*, usually composed of a presbyter, a married couple and a single man, or a presbyter, a single man and a single woman, to be sent to distant dioceses to begin and to guide the implementation of the Neocatechumenal Way.

§ 3. In these *convivences*, which begin with a day of conversion, the international Responsible Team of the Way, or another one designated by it, verifies the availability and coordinates the activity of the itinerants, in a dynamic of "systole" and "diastole" following the example of the Lord who sent his disciples in mission and then gathered them, in a secluded place, to listen to the mighty deeds that the Holy Spirit worked through them.[127]

§ 4. The itinerant catechist remains united to his own parish and community, to which he returns regularly, in order to take part in the Way of his own community. Moreover, the itinerant catechist accepts to live his personal mission in precariousness – according to the praxis of more than 30 years of the Neocatechumenal Way – remaining free to discontinue it at any moment, informing the Bishop *ad quem* and the international Responsible Team of the Way.

Article 32
[Itinerant presbyters]

In the case of the secular clergy, or members of institutes of consecrated life or societies of apostolic life, these must have the express permission of their own diocesan Bishop or competent religious superior, in the appropriate form to participate as itinerant presbyters. The ordinary, in conjunction with the Bishop who welcomes them, establishes the time frame of the presbyters' availability and, is periodically informed of their activity, and ensures that the material and spiritual conditions of their ministry, lived in the spirit of being itinerant, are according to the provisions of the law.

Article 33
[Families in mission]

§ 1. The implementation of the Neocatechumenal Way may be helped by *families in mission* who, upon the request of the Bishops, establish themselves in de-Christianized zones or where an *implantatio ecclesiae* is necessitated.

---

[127] Cf. Lk 10:1, 24.

§ 2. These families are appointed by the international Responsible Team of the Way in special *convivences* from among those who have freely made themselves available to go anywhere, after having considered, with trust in the Lord, both the need of the Church and the absence of impediments within their own family. They are usually sent out by their own Bishop in a suitable celebration.

§ 3. The family in mission remains united to its own parish and community, to which it returns periodically to take part in the way of its own community. Moreover the family accepts to live its mission in precariousness – helped, if possible, by the community of origin – remaining free to discontinue the mission at any moment.

Title VI
The international Responsible Team of the Way

Article 34
[Current international Responsible Team of the Way]

§ 1. The international Responsible Team of the Way is, for their natural life, composed of Kiko Argüello – who is its responsible – and Carmen Hernández, initiators of the Neocatechumenal Way, and the presbyter Don Mario Pezzi of the diocesan clergy of Rome.

§ 2. After the death of one of the two initiators mentioned in the previous paragraph, the other one remains the responsible of the international team and, after hearing the opinion of the presbyter, will proceed to complete the international team. On the death or resignation of the presbyter, the initiators will select another presbyter, presenting him to the Pontifical Council for the Laity for confirmation.

§ 3. After the death of both initiators, the election of the international Responsible Team of the Way will be done according to the procedure established in the following article.

Article 35

[Election of the international Responsible Team of the Way]

§ 1. The election of the international Responsible Team of the Way will be entrusted to an *Electoral College*, numbering between 80 and 120 persons chosen by the same team. Those making up this college are appointed for life, except in those cases where the international Responsible Team of the Way may deem it necessary, for grave reasons, to make some substitutions. Every five years, the aforesaid team will provide for the substitution of any who through death, retirement or for grave reasons have ceased to be part of the college. The list of the members of the electoral college is deposited with the Pontifical Council for the Laity.

§ 2. The election of the international Responsible Team of the Way will take place as follows:

1st. One month prior to the expiry of its mandate, the electoral college is convoked in a *convivence* by members of the outgoing *international Responsible Team of the Way*, or, in the case of death, by the first on the aforementioned list.

2nd. The college, having reached a *quorum* of at least two-thirds of the members, in the first meeting chooses three people to whom will be entrusted the task of scrutineers and other duties relative to the election. The college will elect from among those present or from other catechists of the Way proposed by them, the members of the team, in accordance with can. 119 of the Code of Canon Law.[128] The first to be elected is the responsible of the team, who must be a layman – married or single – and then, by separate ballots, the other members of the team.

3rd. The composition of the team when the voting is completed must include a presbyter, a married couple and a single man, or a presbyter, a single man and a single woman.

---

[128] Cf. can 924, *C.I.C.*

4th. The confirmation of the election of the team will be requested of the Pontifical Council for the Laity by the responsible according to law.[129] If this confirmation is not forthcoming, the entire team will be reëlected.

§ 3. The international Responsible Team of the Way has a mandate of seven years and may be reëlected several times. After each reëlection, the responsible will request confirmation from the Pontifical Council for the Laity.

§ 4. If during the mandate the responsible dies, the team will be entirely reëlected, according to the procedure indicated in §1 and §2; if one of the other members dies, the substitute will be elected, following the same procedure.

Final Disposition

Any future modifications of this present *Statute* will be submitted for approval to the Pontifical Council for the Laity by the international Responsible Team of the Way, after prior consultation with the electoral college.

---

[129] Cf. can. 179 *C.I.C.*

Part II

Papal Discourse

3

John Paul II: "The Statute: A Clear and Sure Rule of Life"

DISCOURSE WITH THE INITIATORS OF THE NEOCATECHUMENAL WAY, THE ITINERANT CATECHISTS AND PRESBYTERS

Castel Gandolfo, September 21, 2002

Address of Kiko Argüello to the Holy Father

Dearest Father,

It is difficult to find words to express the joy and the consolation that this much desired meeting gives us.

Here with me are teams of itinerant catechists who have come from nations all over the world together with parish priests, presbyters, responsibles and catechists of the oldest communities of Spain, Italy and Paris, from whose zeal has stemmed all the evangelization.

We are glad to be able to thank you personally for the approval of the *Statutes* by the Pontifical Council for the Laity, above all because by them we are recognized for what we are: an itinerary of Catholic formation, a post-baptismal catechumenate which, lived in small communities, helps Christians rediscover and live the immense riches of their Baptism. Some canonists in various commentaries have pointed out how important this approval is for all the Church, since it is the first time that a post-baptismal catechumenate has been recognized and approved.

How much consolation your word has always given us! Already in 1952 you emphasized the need for the Church to reintroduce the catechumenate, and during the Council you contributed in a fundamental way to the rediscovery and the restoration of Christian initiation and of the catechumenate. In this very place, Castel Gandolfo, when you received us the first time 23 years ago, you expressed to us your conviction that, in the face of modern atheism, the baptized needed a catechumenate that could reinforce their faith.

Dear Father, faced with the urgent need for a new evangelization and so complex a situation in the Church, we humbly ask you for a word of confirmation and support for the *Statute*–an invitation to the Bishops and the Episcopal conferences to receive this gift of help for the evangelization in their dioceses without fear, a support which can safeguard the catechetical-liturgical praxis the Way has developed in more than 30 years throughout the world, which has given fruit recognized by you and many Bishops, and the synthesis of which is described in the *Statute*.

We think that one of the greatest gifts the Holy Virgin Mary is giving to the Church today through the Neocatechumenal Way, is to offer to Christians in the parishes and all those who are looking for God, the possibility of living the faith in small communities like the first Christians. The cry "Look how they love one another" must be heard again in the world.

We thank you for the trust that you have shown to me, Carmen and Fr. Mario, in our guidance of this Way. We thank the Holy Virgin Mary above all for the Council, without which we would not have been able to do anything, and for your predecessor Pope Paul VI and yourself, who have given us so much help and support.

Thank you, most blessed Father.

Address of the Holy Father

1. Dear catechists and priests of the Neocatechumenal Way, I am happy to receive you as you come here today to meet the Pope. With affection, I greet and welcome each of you and through you, I greet the entire Neocatechumenal Way, an ecclesial reality that has spread to many countries and is appreciated by many pastors. I thank Mr. Kiko Argüello, the co-founder of the Way with Ms. Carmen Hernández, for his cordial address. With his address, he expressed your faithful attachment to the See of Peter and witnessed to your common love for the Church.

2. How can we fail to thank the Lord for the fruit the Neocatechumenal Way has born in the more than 30 years since it came into being? In a secularized society like ours, where religious indifference is spreading and many live as though God did not exist, there are multitudes who need to rediscover the sacraments of Christian initiation, especially Baptism.

The Way is certainly one of the providential answers to this urgent need. Let us look at your communities: how many have rediscovered the beauty and greatness of the baptismal vocation they have received! How much generosity and zeal they have for proclaiming the Gospel of Jesus Christ, especially to those who are the most distant! How many vocations to the priesthood and to the religious life have arisen thanks to this itinerary of Christian formation!

3. I have a vivid memory of our last meeting in January 1997, immediately after your gathering on Mount Sinai to commemorate the 30th anniversary of the Neocatechumenal Way. On that occasion I told you that drafting the Statutes of the Way was *"a very important step that [would] lead to its formal juridical recognition by the Church, and [give] you a further guarantee of the authenticity of your charism"* (*Address to Neocatechumenal Way,* Jan. 24, 1997, n. 4; *OR English,* Feb. 5, 1997, p. 9).

Our meeting today expresses your joy over the recent approval of the Statutes of the Neocatechumenal Way by the Holy See. I am glad that this process, which began more than five years ago, has been brought to completion through an intense effort of consultation, reflection and dialogue. I want now to mention in a special way Cardinal James Francis Stafford, to whom I express my gratitude for the commitment and care with which the Pontifical Council for the Laity accompanied the international leadership team of the Way in this process.

4. I would like to emphasize the importance of the recently approved Statutes for the present and future life of the Neocatechumenal Way. Indeed, above all, this norm stresses once again the ecclesial character of the Neocatechumenal Way which, as I said a few years ago, is "an effective means of Catholic formation for society and for the present time" (Papal Letter *Ogniqualvolta* to Bishop Paul Joseph Cordes, Vice-president of the Pontifical Council for the Laity [today Archbishop and President of the Pontifical Council "Cor Unum"], Aug. 30, 1990; *OR English*, 7, Aug. 14, 1990, p. 4).

The Statutes of the Neocatechumenal Way also describe the essential aspects of this itinerary, offered to the faithful in their parish communities who want to revive their faith, and to adults who are preparing to receive the sacrament of Baptism. Above all, however, the Statutes establish the fundamental tasks of the various persons responsible for providing this itinerary of formation in the Neocatechumenal Communities: the priests, the catechists, the families on mission and the teams responsible at every level. Thus the Statutes must be for the Neocatechumenal Way a "clear and sure rule of life" (*Letter to Cardinal James F. Stafford*, April 5, 2001, n. 2; *OR English*, May 2, 2001, p. 5), a fundamental point of reference so that this process of formation, that aims to bring the faithful to a mature faith, may be realized in a way that is in accord with the teaching and discipline of the Church.

5. The approval of the Statutes marks the beginning of a new phase in the life of the Way. The Church now expects of you an even greater and more generous dedication to the new evangelization and to the service of the local churches and parishes. Therefore, priests and catechists of the Way, you are responsible for ensuring that the Statutes are faithfully put into practice in all their aspects so that they become true leaven for a new missionary

zeal.

The Statutes are likewise an important help to all the pastors of the Church, particularly the diocesan Bishops who are entrusted with the pastoral care and, especially, the Christian initiation of the people in their diocese "in their fatherly and careful accompaniment of the Neocatechumenal Communities" (*Decree of the Pontifical Council for the Laity*, June 29, 2002; *OR English*, July 31, 2002, p. 11). The diocesan ordinaries will be able to find in the Statutes the basic principles for realizing the Neocatechumenal Way in fidelity to its original plan.

I particularly desire to address a word to you priests, who are dedicated to the service of the Neocatechumenal Communities. Never forget that as ministers of Christ you have an irreplaceable role of sanctification, teaching and pastoral guidance for those who follow the itinerary of the Way. With love and generosity, serve the communities entrusted to you!

6. Dear brothers and sisters, with the approval of the Statutes of the Neocatechumenal Way, we have happily succeeded in defining the essential ecclesial formula of the Way. Let us all thank the Lord for this.

It is now the task of the competent offices of the Holy See to examine the Catechetical Directory and the catechetical and liturgical practices of the Way. I am sure that its members willingly and generously support the directives they will receive from these authoritative sources.

I shall continue eagerly to follow your work in the Church and in my prayers I entrust you to the Blessed Virgin Mary, Star of the New Evangelization, and to you I cordially impart my Apostolic Blessing.

The address of the Holy Father is taken from *L'Osservatore Romano*, English edition, Oct. 2, 2002.

Part III

Commentaries on the Day of the Approval

Pontifical Council for the Laity
Aula Magna
Rome, June 28, 2002

4

Address by Kiko Argüello

(28 June 2002)

We are happy that after all the work of these past years it has been possible to arrive at the approval of the *Statute*.

Therefore we can do no less than thank first of all the Holy Father who was the first person to want this approval. Second, we thank his Eminence Cardinal Stafford, who has always been very paternal towards us. I also thank Monsignor Ryłko who has had the patience to bear with our sins and who has given us a truly Christian witness. I also thank the Under-secretary, Dr. Guzman Carriquiri, and the Canonist, Fr. Miguel Delgado, who with great love have accompanied us in the drafting of these Statutes.

In our first meeting with John Paul II at Castel Gandolfo on Sept. 5, 1979, at which Carmen, Fr. Mario and I were present, after the Mass the Pope told us that during the celebration he had seen before him the words: ATHEISM – BAPTISM – CATECHUMENATE.

At that moment I did not understand exactly what this meant, for it seemed almost wrong to me to put Baptism before the catechumenate. The catechumenate, in the tradition of the Church, is for those who are preparing to receive Baptism.

Today, 23 years later, in the face of these Statutes desired by the Pope who personally insisted they be approved, these words have taken on their true meaning.

We can find the key in what the Pope said in a parish in Rome, when he spoke to the Neocatechumenal Communities: "*I see here the genesis of the Neocatechumenate: someone—I don't know if it was Kiko or someone else—has asked himself: Where did the strength of the early Church come from? And from where comes the weakness of the Church today, which has much bigger numbers? And I believe that he has found the answer in the catechumenate, in this Way.*"

When the Pope told us he had seen in front of his eyes the words ATHEISM – BAPTISM – CATECHUMENATE, what did he mean?

I think that having grown up experiencing the atheism of Poland, he, a philosopher whose roots are in the phenomenology of Husserl, meant that to answer the power of modern atheism and the forces of secularization, baptized Christians need a catechumenate like that which existed in the primitive Church—a post-baptismal catechumenate.

This is the basis of the approval of the Statutes of the Neocatechumenal Way, not as an association, but as a post-baptismal catechumenate, as a Christian initiation, an instrument that the Holy See offers to the Bishops so that, in response to modern atheism, the Baptism of Christians can be strengthened.

In the VI Symposium of European Bishops in 1985, after having seriously examined the current secularization which ravages the roots of faith, he, a modern man who suffers when he sees society lacerated by the destruction of the family, said: "The Holy Spirit has already given an answer to the situation. We have to go where the Spirit is working, and showing us signs of life. We have to have the courage to leave behind our atrophied schemes and welcome the new realities that the Holy Spirit is creating...."

Juridically speaking, the fulcrum of Christian initiation is the Bishop, thus Canon 788 of the Code of Canon Law says that it is the task of Episcopal conferences to issue Statutes which regulate Christian initiation.

So today almost all Episcopal conferences speak about the need for a post-baptismal initiation. And they find it very difficult to put this into practice.

With these Statutes, the Pope courageously offers a means of initiation and a post-baptismal catechumenate validated by more than 30 years of a Way which has produced many fruits.

We can only thank the blessed Virgin Mary who inspired this Way leading us to make communities like the Holy Family of Nazareth, which live in humility, simplicity and praise, where the other is Christ.

This is the passage from a pastoral work of Christianity, or we could say, of a Christianity of the temple, to the pastoral work of the community as the body of the risen Christ.

During its first three centuries, the primitive Church had a serious catechumenate where, before receiving Baptism, the catechumens had to show that they had faith, that they had begun to do the works of life – those which evidenced that the risen Christ lived in them.

Here we can see that Baptism was the gestation of a new creation, where the synthesis of the announcement of the kerygma, the Good News, the change of moral life and the liturgy were one single thing.

These Christians were inserted in living communities. They met in their houses; God himself placed these communities on a lamp stand and, through persecution, they were able to show the signs of the new man announced by the Sermon on the Mount: *"Do not resist evil, if anyone strikes you on the right cheek, offer him the left; and if anyone takes you to court to steal your tunic, give him your cloak as well, and if anyone steals what is yours, do not ask for it back; love your enemies, do good to those who hate you."*

Here are the signs of the crucified Christ: love "as I have loved you," by this love they will know that you are my disciples; "be perfectly one and the world will believe."

These communities converted the Roman empire; today in front of globalization, atheism and the apostasy of Europe, here is John Paul II saying that we need to return to the primitive model.

But for us there is only one point: that the new man, the heavenly man, may appear, in a serious itinerary of Christian formation; that man who like Saint Paul says, carries in his body the dying of Jesus, so that in his body it can be made manifest that Christ is alive, in such a way that when the Christian dies "the world receives life."

With these Statutes, the Pope recognizes the Neocatechumenal Way as an itinerary of Catholic formation valid for our society and times, and wishes that the Bishops and their priests value and help this work for the new evangelization so that it may be carried out according to the guidelines proposed by the initiators. With *these Statutes, the guidelines of the initiators are made concrete* as a "clear and certain rule" for the Bishops in their work of evangelization, in the mandate to evangelize all nations that they have received from Christ.

In these years, seeing the witness of many brothers and sisters in these communities, we have encountered many pagans who have desired to draw closer to Christ and have asked to be baptized. We have welcomed them in our communities and accompanied them for four years in their itinerary of the RCIA, with marvelous fruits.

This reality is also recognized in these Statutes, which will be welcomed with great joy by many pagans who are drawing near our communities. We are happy to be of service to Bishops and pastors without trying to establish any parallel structures.

From a juridical point of view, these Statutes, without a doubt, are a novelty, but we hope that they will be welcomed with joy by pastors and Bishops and that they will help to dispel misunderstandings and prejudices, which are often a result of lack of knowledge of the Way.

Carmen and Fr. Mario join me in extending our thanks to all of you.

Pray for me, a sinner.

Ad Maiorem Dei Gloriam

June 29, 2002
Solemnity of SS. Peter and Paul

5

Address by Carmen Hernández

Do you know how I would like to begin in front of this Virgin who presides over us? *"Magnificat anima mea Dominum,* my spirit exults in God my Savior!" With this I'm taken back to Ein Karem where I arrived, by the grace of the Lord, after an enormous *kenosis,* which I lived in 1962, during which I went up to Mount Moriah with my Isaac, going up to Mount Moriah with my Isaac which was my missionary vocation, by which I was ready and prepared to go to India – and then I had to return home, like Jacob.

I'm happy that today is Friday and that the feast of Saint Peter and Saint Paul falls on Saturday, because also this brings me to Vatican II and the Paschal Triduum.

I thank you, Ryłko and this Council who have suffered with us. But, above all, I thank Msgr. Farnés who is here and I also congratulate him, because he is called Peter. In 1961, young and handsome, Farnés came from the Liturgical Institute in Paris with a doctorate in liturgy and lived all the preparation of the Council with Dom Botte (he really is a son of Dom Botte), with Bouyer, with the great ones who prepared all the liturgical renewal of the Council.

To be brief, in an airplane hijacking which the Lord did to me, and I found myself in Barcelona instead of India. Fr Farnés was then in Barcelona. There is a marvelous museum there, the Mares museum, which has a collection of Romanesque crucifixes.

I went there many times and cried seeing Jesus Christ judged in the name of the law, but really triumphant on the Cross.

I had a great devotion to the Eucharist. By the grace of the Lord, dead or alive, I never missed communion. I would get up in the morning and before rushing off to the university I did–in "Jesuit" style–my hour's adoration of Jesus Christ before Mass. During this time, God, through the Eucharist, freed me from lots of my problems. Even when I traveled with my father to Rabat or Casablanca, or other such places where it was difficult to find a church, I was always able to find a mass so I could attend communion. I wouldn't miss Communion for anything in the world because for me it was the Presence of Jesus Christ, which truly helped me. Later, through another significant *kenosis* in my life, there in Barcelona, thanks to Father Farnés, God opened my ear to understand what the Second Vatican Council meant.

There is not only this presence of Jesus Christ who comes to visit your heart and help you, what becomes present to you is the Lord's Resurrection from death where Christ invites you to enter into death with him to rise again with him. There is a dynamic, a song to the Resurrection. In order to express this, a community is needed. The Council did all this as a renewal. This was the SUN OF THE RESURRECTION, which at that time was still clouded over by a series of medieval interpretations. The Council, going back to the origins, unveiled the force of the Passover, of that night of vigil which is a passage to the light of the resurrection, and how important it is that Jesus Christ went down to Egypt and came out of Egypt, passing from slavery to freedom.

This for me was a great paschal discovery which I arrived at in 1961 because of Mgsr. Farnés. It really was a direct result of the renewal of the Second Vatican Council which allowed the liturgy to flourish with a striking paschal splendor.

Reading something written by Wojtyla in 1952 when he was still a priest, you can understand how he lived. I don't know how or in what way, he came to these insights about the power of the Passover night–the night of light, the night of water–and how important Baptism by immersion is for really signifying the passage of the Red Sea during this unique, marvelous night which illumines all of liturgy. At this time he also proposed the catechumenate for the 20th century. This sensitivity of the Pope moves me because he feels it so strongly that even now, even as sick as he is, he celebrated the Passover night, and with Baptisms.

And after Christmas, on the feast of St John "he went down to the Jordan to baptize children" and he did it in the Sistine chapel with all the families and the babies who cried. And I see him with an enormous strength.

This is why, before everything else, I thank God who is immense and who founded his Church on the rock, on Peter. For in the midst of these great sufferings I had in Barcelona in which I discovered the Passover, God brought me to the land of Israel, where I traveled throughout without money or any support – from Tripoli in Lebanon, where there is a Sanctuary and many cedars, down to the Negeb and as far as Eilat on the Red Sea. You couldn't get to Sinai in those days. I traveled on foot through all that land and God opened the Scriptures for me in an impressive way. I thank the Lord for this experience.

One of the strongest graces I've received was at Ein Karem. With some friends, I had been thinking about founding a new association or a movement, but from Our Lady I heard: "No... it's the Church: *Blessed are you among women.* It will be the Church." In the midst of a thousand problems, I often went to the rock of the Primacy. At that time there weren't so many tourists. It was like now, with problems. There was still the wall in Jerusalem. I would go to the Primacy of Peter and there I spent hours and days sitting on the rock, asking God what my place was in the Church. For this reason, when I came back from Israel I went first of all to St Peter's and prayed the Creed there; then I went to St Paul's. This is why it moves me that this Decree is being signed on the day of Saints Peter and Paul, for after my experience I have watched all the communities go there and then proceeding on to the Holy Land, where God had prepared me.

I am very fond of Kiko Argüello, who is an artist. I got to know him by chance, because he was working with one of my sisters (helping prostitutes and homosexuals). Going to Madrid was the last thing I wanted to do. My father was an industrialist, handling enormous projects who had made me study science and chemistry. He told me: "Working with your father you'll be able to do more for the missions..." So I had little desire to go to Madrid [Kiko is already interrupting me, as usual. When I begin to talk, Kiko interrupts me].

God did not prepare me with the theater, but with science and chemistry, and gave me enormous graces. So, as I was mentioning, I met Kiko through my sister who told me, "I've met a messianic type like yourself. You must get to know him." Thus we agreed to meet at the Cibeles Plaza, in a bar facing the post office. He was half an hour late and, after our conversation, when he had to leave, he asked me for a thousand pesetas to pay for the taxi. Can you believe this? After this first meeting with Kiko we again met at a bar in Palomeras. Some friends and I wanted to establish a new foundation together. I had already lived with the poor in Barcelona in 1964 – which I mention because even though this 1964 date is a valid beginning point, for me the Way began with the Second Vatican Council. [Don't interrupt me, Kiko, because I have to tell my experience before Holy Mother Church.]

Well, in that bar in Palomeras Altas, I looked at Kiko a bit askance, because I came from great sufferings and he seemed to me to be a youngster full of the Cursillos movement ... and he told me that he had had a vision of Our Lady who had told him to *make communities like that of the Holy Family of Nazareth*. Even though I had spent a long time in Nazareth and in the grotto before the church was built there, I had never felt the significance of St. Joseph. I felt Our Lady and the announcement of the Gospel, the evangelization very strongly, but not St Joseph. So when Kiko began to talk about the Family of Nazareth, I thought, "This is a young Cursillist bigot." Later I saw how God had led Kiko to this idea of the "small community," which I had so often tried to make in other places before the shantytown, but had never been able to. In the shantytown he "encountered" the Council, thanks to me. I always say that I handed him the Council on a silver platter, in the midst of never-ending struggles. It was a struggle to the death to get him to progress from the Servant of Yahweh – which is true – and from the Cross to the Resurrection. This is why the first song he wrote is "The Servant of Yahweh" and the last, after great battles, after having lived the Passover night, is "He Rose from Death." Here with us is a witness to all these happenings: José Agudo, one of the first of the shantytown, with his wife Rosario, who is a true gypsy. They have 15 children.

Father, the marvel was that Msgr. Morcillo, the Archbishop of Madrid, at a very important moment, came to the shantytown. At that moment I really began to collaborate with Kiko, because I had done various things independently of him. The Church always helped us. I could tell you many stories about Paul VI and how the Church has always helped us. Today I thank the Lord that I am in the Church.

For me the Statutes are a scaffolding; the important thing is to be in the Church. Fundamentally, this scaffolding will contribute to the renewal of the Church which the Council wanted, so that the Church really is a light which illumines globalization and the young people's problems that we are seeing. Youth follows this old Pope who has an enormous power of attraction because he represents Peter. I am happy with today's reading: "You are Peter and upon this rock I will build my Church." This has always been for me an immovable faith. I could care less about Kiko, but I care that this is in the Church. Kiko and I will pass away, as everything passes, as all the congregations pass away, but the Church remains. The Church will not pass away, with its baptismal font of renewal and with the sun of the resurrection, towards which history is walking. This very day we are flying in space, for the earth is not still. The universe is on a marvelous voyage in the light. Physics today says that we are moving towards the light Thus today's reading moves me: "You are Peter." Do you know what happens six days after this Gospel in Ceasarea Philippi, where this gospel takes place? The transfiguration!

[Father, you see that Kiko never lets me speak!] Our Lady doesn't speak, but at Pentecost she is more important than all the apostles.

Good, I thank everyone, especially Msgr. Ryłko because the battle we fought was very interesting. He had an enormous desire to help us, it's true, and for him the real help was to make us safe in an association. The struggle we had was good for him and us, and also for this Pontifical Council for the Laity, which will have an immense future, giving support to the Neocatechumenal way.

In this battle I recall many things of our history, because I saw that it was not we, neither Kiko nor I, but God, who was acting in history and through Peter. We have recently returned from China, Father, we see how God provides. There he put a family whom we didn't prepare, who knows Chinese and who is already doing marvelous things in the evangelization. God is preparing Russia too in the same way. We have seen miracle after miracle.

Thank you to Msgr. Ryłko. Many times it seemed to me that Msgr. Stafford didn't understand. We knew him from Denver and were fond of him. I thank him because he visited me in hospital when I was sick. He promised me financial help for the "Domus Galilaeae," but hasn't given me a dollar! I'm still waiting! Thanks, too, to Carriquiry who had immense patience and who with a drawn sword kept up the battle with us, while Ryłko was in the background. We must also thank Dr. Miguel Delgado of Opus Dei who helped us very much. When I was young and studying chemistry I had a friend in Opus Dei who wanted me to join them. But I wanted to go on the missions and so I didn't join Opus Dei but I knew Father Escrivá de Balaguer and Father Marcelino Olaechea.

Do you know for what else I have to give thanks? That we have not fallen into *"kikianism"*! The real danger was not Msgr. Ryłko with the association, for me the danger is Kiko Argüello. We don't want to die "kikos." We are a Christian initiation in the Church, therefore we are in the Church! And Kiko can die with all his *"kikianism"* and his songs, but the baptismal pool will go on pouring out water because "You are Peter and upon this rock I will build my Church," where I want to be.

To conclude I say with St Teresa: Thank you for allowing me to die in the Church.

6

Address by Fr. Mario Pezzi

I will be brief: Our Lord Jesus Christ spoke a lot, Our Lady spoke little. With respect to St. Joseph, the Pope says in *Redemptoris Custos* that he didn't speak much but did what the Lord told him to do, and this is why I will say very little. I am very grateful, happy and grateful to the Lord, and I bless him for this day, for this recognition.

I too have a whole history. I still remember Pius XII, who in his Christmas talks spoke about a springtime in the Church. I was young at the time, but it struck me. Then I closely followed the way the Second Vatican Council evolved. Here in Rome I could follow at *Propaganda Fide* all the spirit of renewal of the Council. Before being ordained and coming to know Kiko and Carmen, I lived through a time of interior turmoil. It was the period of 1968-69 when I saw this distance between the presbyter and the people of God, this language which did not reach the people, a liturgy which did not affect the life of the people. I had a relative who for reasons of inheritance hadn't set foot in his parents' house for 40 years. He had stopped talking to his mother because of money, yet he went to mass every Sunday. For me this was a cause of scandal – and I looked for the answers that the Council gave. But I questioned whether it was possible to put it into practice. My spiritual director was providential for me. He said, "Don't take any step until God has shown you his will. When he shows it to you, he will do so with clarity and peace." I lived through six troubled years. I accepted ordination because I felt the vocation, but I didn't know how things would turn out for me. Six months after being ordained, I got to know Kiko and Carmen, the Neocatechumenal Way, and I found the answer.

Today is an important day for me, because during all these 30 years in which we have seen marvels – I have been a witness with Kiko and Carmen. I'm not an initiator, I was called to collaborate with them as a presbyter – we have seen marvels: we have been comforted, above all, by the Holy Father, by many Bishops, we've also had many sufferings. Sometimes, I was discouraged, thinking "How is it possible that the Church does not realize the urgency and the need there is for a catechumenate?" I was intended for Africa, a missionary of the Comboni Fathers, and I followed this Way thinking that the catechumenate was essential because in Africa we have had tragedies. In Burundi, for example, where there was a flourishing Catholicism we have seen a civil war break out where Christians were killing and massacring each other. This created a crisis in many missionaries who lost their faith because a serious and profound initiation was missing. I said that the Way helps, as we see in Congo and in our communities in Africa today. And finally I see that the Lord is faithful, that the Church really is a mother.

I ask Msgr. Ryłko for forgiveness because I irritated him many times; and also to all of you. Today I see the Church is a mother and that the word of the Gospel is fulfilled: "Neither flesh nor blood has revealed this to you, but my Father." And for me, too, this is a security: "You are Peter and upon this rock I will build my Church." Being confirmed by Peter gives us more vigor, confirms us in the mission with which we have been entrusted and helps us bear the crosses which await us. This is what I think.

7

Address by Card. James Francis Stafford

Good. Thank you. I well remember the first time I had the opportunity to meet the members of the Neocatechumenal Communities in 1990, here in Rome during the Synod of Bishops. On that occasion I thought this was something new emerging from the Council, a new phenomenon in the Church as well as a great blessing for the Church. And now we find ourselves at this incredible point, this great blessing is a grace for me and also for all of you. *Deo gratias*!

Dear friends, in the name of the Pontifical Council for the Laity, I want first of all to greet the international Responsible Team for the Neocatechumenal Way: Kiko, Carmen and Mario. Cordially, sincerely, with all my heart, I extend a welcome to all of you who have come to this ceremony. Certainly you all will remember with joy the unforgettable audience granted to you by the Holy Father on January 24, 1997, after the meeting at Mount Sinai commemorating 30 years of life of the Way. On that occasion, as we have already heard, Pope John Paul II said that drawing up the *Statute of the Way* was "*a very important step which opens the way towards its formal juridical recognition by the Church, giving you a further guarantee of the authenticity of your charism,*" and he encouraged you to carry out this work under the guidance of the Pontifical Council for the Laity. A further confirmation of this wish can be found in the Autograph letter from the pontiff to me on April 5, 2001, in which he confirms the competence of this

Dicastery to bring to completion the approval of the *Statute of the Neocatechumenal Way*, at the same time entrusting to us the task of accompanying you in the future.

The handing over of the Decree of approval of your *Statute* is a very significant occasion not only for you, but also for this Dicastery and for the universal Church. The Pontifical Council for the Laity is happy to have collaborated with the international Responsible Team in drawing up a basic normative framework, which in the future can guide the functioning of the Neocatechumenal Way in the Church. Before anything else we must thank the Lord, three times holy, from whom all good things come, because he has always guided the work undertaken five years ago allowing us to bring this taxing process to its best conclusion. In the first reading we have just listened to, the Apostle Paul addresses himself to the inhabitants of Corinth recounting the historical facts of the Resurrection of Jesus – a fundamental truth of our faith and at the same time a decisive proof of his divinity. The resurrection of Jesus and his subsequent appearances to Peter, the apostles and to others have a transcendental importance. In fact, this is how all these people became the first witnesses of the resurrection of Jesus, since this announcement – as we see in the discourses of St. Peter and St. Paul in the Acts of the Apostles – is pivotal for the apostolic catechesis. It should also be noted how St. Paul's self-abasement – he says he is like a child untimely born – makes the action of God's grace possible. We Christians too, moved by the shining example left us throughout the history of Christianity by the Apostles and by many disciples of Jesus, must be faithful witnesses of Christ along all the roads of this world which is in continuous need of his message.

In the apostolic letter *Novo millennio ineunte*, the Holy Father writes: "Over the years I have often repeated the summons to the *new* evangelization. I do so again now, especially in order to insist that we must rekindle in ourselves the impetus of the beginning and allow ourselves to be filled with the ardor of the apostolic preaching which followed Pentecost. We must revive in ourselves the burning conviction of Paul, who cried out: 'Woe to me if I do not preach the Gospel.'" In complete harmony with what the Holy Father affirms, I know well how you have taken to heart the expression "new evangelization." The Church counts a great deal on you, as lay faithful, to carry out this goal for the parishes (this is important): to evangelize the world as the first Christians did, conscious of the great responsibility involved in becoming disciples of Christ with the reception of the sacrament of Baptism. In our days this is not just a beautiful ideal, but a tangible task which God entrusts to all the baptized and to all parishes. In this sense an important help for the new evangelization is represented by the rediscovery of the riches of Christian initiation, which through the itinerary of the neocatechumenate is offered to Christians – some of whom live as though they had not been baptized. And not just some; many live like this! You, too, are committed to an adequate preparation for the Baptism of adult Christians. This is a great need in the Church for the world of our times.

We have also listened to the Gospel of tomorrow's Mass, the solemnity of the holy apostles Peter and Paul. Jesus promises Peter the primacy of the Church after the apostle's profession of faith near Caesarea Philippi. It is very significant, as St. John relates, that the primacy is conferred on Peter after the resurrection of Jesus. This teaches us that the Church is founded on the rock that is Peter, the solid rock that is Peter. And in his successors it will remain firm until the end of time.

Next Sunday I will have the joy of addressing all the catechists who are gathered at Porto S. Giorgio for this event which is so significant for the Neocatechumenal Way. Now I only want to say that, respecting completely your ecclesial identity and your particular apostolic procedures, it is necessary that you always work in complete harmony with the Vicar of Christ, as well as with the individual diocesan Bishops in their capacity as pastors of the local churches. This is the guarantee of the authenticity of your commitment to the service of the universal Church. I am thinking of the example of St. Francis of Assisi and his relationship with the Bishops and Popes of the Church of his time. Today a new stage in the history of the Neocatechumenal Way is beginning, in which your relationship with the See of Peter is forged even closer. The *Statute* which will govern the life of the Way has been approved *ad experimentum* for an initial period of five years. At the end of this period, with the experience acquired, you will seek further confirmation from the Dicastery. Today's event is not a point of arrival, but rather a point of departure for the Way, from this place which is your house. The next step to be undertaken, as you well know, is the approval of the Catechetical Directory. In this process the Pontifical Council for the Laity will be close with you, committed to accompanying you with solicitude. I am sure that you will never lack the intercession of Our Lady, Mary, little Mary – this "little Mary" is very beautiful – as you sang at the beginning, for the generous service you offer to the Church. May God bless you always with fruits of holiness and evangelization.

8

Address of Card. James Francis Stafford to the Itinerant Catechists

(Porto San Giorgio, Sunday, June 30, 2002)

It is a great joy to be with you here in Porto San Giorgio – itinerant catechists from all continents who are gathered in prayer, praising God and thanking him for the approval of the *Statute of the Neocatechumenal Way* by the Pontifical Council for the Laity. In fact, on June 28 I put into the hands of Kiko Argüello, Carmen Hernández and Fr. Mario Pezzi the Decree of approval of the *Statute*, bearing the date of June 29, Solemnity of Sts. Peter and Paul, that I signed as President of the council along with Archbishop Stanisław Ryłko, Secretary of the council.

Ecclesial Meaning of Act of Approval

Of course, it was a juridical act, but it also has profound ecclesial meaning. You should be convinced of it for one would be mistaken to think that the approval of the *Statute* was merely a bureaucratic measure. Rather, it satisfies a deep desire of the Holy Father, which he expressed publicly at the meeting with you on January 24, 1997 – as you well remember – and repeated to me in the Autograph letter he sent me on April 5, 2001, confirming the mandate of the Pontifical Council for the Laity to complete the delicate process of the discernment and approval of the *Statute*, as one of the "unavoidable provisions" for the "existence of the Way" (*Letter to Cardinal Stafford, President of the Pontifical Council for the Laity*; ORE, May 2, 2001, p. 5).

Three Main Points

Today, my brief discourse will deal with three main points: first, the great gift that the Neocatechumenal Way is for the Church; second, the importance of the process of the drafting of the *Statute* and the *Statute* itself; and third, four areas that require special attention in the life of the Way: the relationship with the Bishops, priests and all the dimensions of the parish and other ecclesial communities, as well as scrupulous respect for the individual's freedom with a special emphasis on the "internal forum."

Abundant Fruits of the Way

On many occasions, the Holy Father has underlined the abundant fruits of conversion, mature faith, fraternal communion and missionary zeal of the Neocatechumenal Communities, recognizing the Way as "an effective means of Catholic formation for society and for the present time" (AAS 82 [1990-II] 1513-1515). Nor should I fail to mention the words the Pope addressed to you on the 30th anniversary of the Way: "How far you have come with the Lord's help! In recent years the Way has realized a truly impressive growth and spread in the Church like the mustard seed of the Gospel, a great tree which has now spread to more than 100 countries of the world...." Then the Pope underscored "the abundant gifts that in these years the Lord has granted to you, and through you, to the whole Church." In his address, the Pope mentioned your flourishing development in terms of the blossoming of charisms and new ways of expressing the Church as the mystery of missionary communion (cf. John Paul II, *Address to members of the Neocatechumenal Way*, Jan. 24, 1997; ORE, Feb. 5, 1997).

Drafting, Approval of Statute: Sure Rule of Life

To this encouraging recognition, however, a concrete response had to be given: namely, the examination and consequent approval of the *Statute of the Way*. Since this movement is as varied as it is complex, consisting of Neocatechumenal Communities in a multitude of dioceses and parishes in many different countries, with the work of the itinerant catechists and mission families, plus the existence of more than 40 *Redemptoris Mater* diocesan seminaries connected with the experience of the Way, how could this all happen without a clear and sure "light and rule of life" (cf. *Signed Letter* n. 2), to be translated into the drafting of normative Statutes? If the Way were based solely on oral tradition, did it not risk being indefinite, putting everything at the mercy of possible arbitrary decisions due to the lack of certain guidelines that everyone would accept and respect? Today these normative Statutes approved by the Holy See – as it clearly says in the Decree – constitute firm and reliable guidelines for the life of the Way.

Initiators' Five-Year Dialogue with the Council

The initiators of the Way became increasingly aware of the importance of having Statutes. Along with some collaborators, they were involved in an ongoing dialogue with our Council, to achieve the goal pointed out by the Holy Father for the good of the Church and, especially, of the Neocatechumenal Way. For more than five years I have been involved in examining the various versions and successive drafts of the Statutes that they submitted to the Pontifical Council for the Laity. The dialogue was lively, at times even difficult, but was always guided by a deep sense of ecclesial consciousness and charity. During these years, the Pontifical Council for the Laity has always worked in close collaboration with the other departments of the Roman Curia directly interested in this matter, by reason of their particular area of responsibility.

Roman Curia Contributed Greatly

The Congregation for the Doctrine of the Faith made some valuable observations which were duly incorporated into the definitive text. In recent years, we have been in frequent contact with the individual Bishops and Bishops' conferences around the world to evaluate the experience of the Way at local, diocesan and national levels. Many Patriarchs, Cardinals and Bishops have written to the Holy Father to encourage the examination and approval of the *Statute*. For our part, we have frequently consulted canonical experts, and have not neglected to weigh carefully the large number of other reports and observations from those with firsthand experience of the Way.

This long process of elaboration and examination of the Statutes was both a providential opportunity and an important time for the discernment by the Holy See of the message and experience of the Neocatechumenal Way. It culminates in this "further guarantee of the authenticity of your charism" (cf. John Paul II, *Address to the Neocatechumenal Way*, 24 January 1997, *op. cit.*, *Autograph Letter*, *op. cit.*, n. 2) that is the approval of the Statutes.

Respect for the reality of the Way

The initiators of the Way, and those who assisted them during this process, can testify to the great determination with which the Pontifical Council for the Laity proceeded to fulfil the Holy Father's mandate within the sphere of its own responsibility and the care and respect with which it worked so that the reality of the Way might be respected, in accord with the guidelines proposed by its initiators. In fact, our Council is not entitled to work out or impose normative Statutes on the different realities that enjoy the freedom to express in the Statutes that they submit to the Holy See, their own charism, aims, pedagogy, "style" and specific procedures and ways of working. In the case of the Neocatechumenal Way, the participation of the ecclesiastical authorities was limited to verifying and ensuring the conformity of the Statutes with the doctrine and discipline of the Church.

This was done to ensure that the experience of the Way would bear even greater fruit of the "Gospel radicalism and extraordinary missionary zeal that it brings to the life of the lay faithful, to families, to parish communities, and the abundance of vocations it inspires to the priestly and religious life" (cf. *Decree of the Pontifical Council for the Laity*, 29 June 2002), and that this good fruit would be ever more deeply rooted in the fertile soil of the Catholic Church.

Safeguards Proposed by Holy See

At the same time, the Holy See insisted on some fundamental aspects which I would like to call to your attention. The relations of Christians with one another are governed by the great law St. Paul gave us: "Be subject to one another out of reverence for

Christ" (Eph 5:21). This doctrinal and moral principle, rooted in the dignity of every baptized person, governs relations between all Christians. In the last part of the fifth chapter of his letter, St. Paul applies this principle to the special relations existing in the life of the Church.

Mission of the Local Bishops

The first catechists in the Church are the Bishops, successors of the Apostles, consecrated by God and assisted by the Holy Spirit so that they may be good shepherds of their flocks, the heads of the different local Churches. Consequently, they are charged with the delicate and pressing responsibility of proclaiming Christ's Gospel, of being stewards of the divine mysteries, of teaching the truth of the faith and sound doctrine, and of presiding over the faithful, gathered in the unity of charity. Therefore you must always defer respectfully and obediently to the Bishops united with the Holy Father in the Apostolic College. Do nothing without the Bishop! The Statuted are offered to Bishops – as the Decree states – as an "important aid" in their "fatherly and careful guidance of the Neocatechumenal Communities" (cf. *Decree of the Pontifical Council for the Laity*, June 29, 2002).

The Statutes are an instrument at the service of communion, hence, they are also an "instrument at the service of the Bishops" (cf. art. 5 of the *Statute*). We are pleased to recall and to apply here what the Holy Father said in his encyclical letter *Redemptoris Missio*, (n. 72) when he requested the Bishops to give a cordial and generous welcome to the new ecclesial movements present in their dioceses and asked of these movements a true spirit of humility in proposing and following their itinerary, as they integrate themselves into the living, manifold fabric of Christian communities.

It is true that the approval of the Statutes on the part of the Holy See is an invitation and a guarantee that the experience of the Way will continue to develop in many new dioceses, as the Statutes themselves say, affirming that it is up to each Bishop "to authorize the introduction of the Neocatechumenal Way in the diocese" (art. 26) so that it may go forward in the parishes to which it has been expressly invited. The Statutes thus invest the Bishops with a great responsibility. "Be subject to one another out of reverence for Christ": this principle governs relations between the Bishops and all those who belong to the Way.

Appreciate the Mission of the Parish Priest, the Vocation of Clerics and Religious

The Holy See was also concerned in the Statutes to clarify the importance of the mission of the parish priest in the Neocatechumenal Community, appreciating the presence of the priest and his office of governing, teaching and sanctifying; as well as ensuring the proper respect for the vocation of clerics and the discipline of the religious who follow the Way.

Protect the Freedom of the Internal Forum

The strong affirmation of the protection of the "internal forum" of the members was felt as a need. This is not meant to restrict the "way" of conversion according to the proper pedagogy of the community, but rather to guarantee people's free option, while at the same time increasing their appreciation of the sacrament of Penance, in agreement with what the Holy Father recently taught in his *"Motu proprio" Misericordia Dei*. Many are the observations incorporated into the text and in all this I must give credit to the initiators of the Way for having received obediently and intelligently all that was suggested, which in their mind agrees with the true nature and practice of the Way.

Willingness to be Integrated into Parish and Diocesan Communities

I particularly wish to stress the fundamental aspect, represented by your full openness of spirit and effective willingness to be integrated into parish and diocesan communities, not only at the service of those who follow the "Way," but of the whole community. You offer the gifts and talents the Lord has given you, while at the same time you appreciate all that the Spirit inspires in the life of the faithful through the different processes of Christian formation and different ways of expressing the mystery of holiness and communion. St. Paul "makes his exhortations, which describe a life imbued with the Spirit, culminate in the invitation addressed to all believers to be subject to one another.... Furthermore, the duties are listed as reciprocal duties: 'Be subject to one another out of reverence for Christ'" (C.S. Keenan).

Now the Application Begins

I entrust these Statutes to each of you, to the responsibility of each one before God. You are all co-responsible for adapting your work to the rule you have been given, whose normative directives are to be fully respected. Indeed, the Statutes have been examined and revised down to the smallest detail: there is a reason for every expression. They must always be for each of you and all of you, an enlightened directive for fruitful growth in the Church and for the Church.

Further Tasks Pending

Of course, one cannot ask everything of the Statutes. Since they are a juridical instrument, they cannot afford a deep systematic orientation for doctrinal, liturgical or catechetical matters. In fact, it is not by chance that the *Statute of the Way* refers explicitly to the Catechetical Directory (*The Neocatechumenal Way: Guidelines for the Teams of Catechists*) whose different volumes you have presented to the congregations responsible – the Congregations for the Doctrine of the Faith, for Divine Worship and the Discipline of the Sacraments and for the Clergy – and are awaiting their examination and joint approval. The approval of the Statutes can be an authoritative and useful support for the work of revision that is under way.

Council Is to Continue its Guidance

Furthermore, the approval of the Statutes has been granted *ad experimentum* for five years. This commits the Pontifical Council for the Laity not only to fulfil carefully the mandate entrusted by the Supreme Pontiff, but also "to continue accompanying the Way in the future" (cf. John Paul II, *Autograph Letter, op. cit.,* n. 3), and continue the dialogue with the initiators of the Way to discern and verify the application of the Statutes to the practice of the Way.

What is truly important is that the Statutes, approved by the Pontifical Council for the Laity in accord with the Holy Father's desire, be for you cause for gratitude, joy, certainty and hope on your journey as well as a reminder of divine Providence to take ever greater responsibility for the gift the Lord has given to you for the sanctification of persons, for the building of Christian communities and for a growing zeal for taking the "new evangelization" to the ends of the earth for the greater glory of God.

The Mystery of the Glorious Cross

All who are acquainted with the Neocatechumenal Way are familiar with the representation of the glorious Cross which some of you even have at home. In the catechesis for the *convivencia* before the first scrutiny, Kiko Argüello proclaims: "The glorious Cross is the profound secret of Christianity.... The Cross is really the way of our salvation."

It is the Cross of Jesus which shapes from within the Decree and the Statutes whose approval we are celebrating today. The mystery of the Cross, into which every Christian has been baptized, is a unique mystery, the mystery of the love of the Father and the Son. Coming to the end of his earthly pilgrimage, the Son abandoned himself with obedient love to his Father: "Father, into your hands I commit my spirit" (Lk 23:46).

In these years during which you will progress together in the application of these Statutes, I ask you to be attentive to all the paths that lead to God, shown by the obedient love of the One who died on the Cross. The acceptance and faithful application of the Statutes, as well as obedience to the Holy Father and to the Bishops of the Church, are essential to the reward promised to those who follow the way of the Beatitudes: "good measure, pressed down, shaken together, running over, will be put into your lap" (Lk 6:38).

Obedient love requires the poverty that permeates the Beatitudes. Through obedient love, you will always be led further into the mystery of the fullness of God's glory, revealed in the Cross of Jesus. All those among you who walk this blessed way will be like the little ones, whose angels constantly look upon the face of the Father. Your own holy simplicity will open up to you God's indivisible simplicity.

Part IV

Juridical and Ecclesial Commentaries on the *Statute*

9

Historical Notes
by Ezechiele Pasotti

In 1964, Francisco (Kiko) Argüello, a painter born in Léon, Spain, and Carmen Hernández, a graduate in chemistry and formed in the institute *Misioneras de Cristo Jesús*, meet in the shantytown of Palomeras Altas on the outskirts of Madrid. After three years, in this milieu of mostly poor people, a kerygmatic-catechetical synthesis began to take shape which, sustained by the Word of God, by the liturgy and by an experience in community – all in the wake of the Second Vatican Council, would become the basis of what the Neocatechumenal Way was to take to the whole world.

From the shantytown the experience soon moves to some parishes in Madrid and Zamora. There the kerygmatic-catechetical synthesis formed among slum dwellers in Palomeras Altas faced a challenge. It was soon seen that, particularly in well-off parishes, the catecheses were used as a way of "dressing up," as conferences, not as a way of conversion and of *kenosis* where little by little the old man is put to death, to be re-clothed in the new creation of the Holy Spirit.

In this manner Baptism gradually appeared as a way to follow in order to arrive at an adult faith able to respond to the social changes which were taking place.

Soon it became clear that there was a need for a first reflection on what was happening and on what the Lord was doing in these communities. In April 1970, at Majadahonda, near Madrid, the initiators of the Way–Kiko and Carmen–with the responsibles, presbyters and some pastors of the existing first communities met to reflect on what the Holy Spirit was doing in their midst. A questionnaire with a basic question was prepared: What are these communities which are being born in the parishes?

After three days of prayer and work the following answer was unanimously arrived at:

What is the community?

- The community is the Church: which is the visible Body of the risen Christ. It is born from the announcement of the "Good News" which is Christ, conqueror of everything in us which kills and destroys us.
- This announcement is apostolic: unity with and dependence on the Bishop, guarantee of truth and universality.
- We are called by God to be sacraments of salvation within the existing parish structure; a way towards adult faith begins, through a catechumenate lived by means of the "tripod": *Word of God, Liturgy and Community.*

Mission of These Communities Within the Existing Church Structure

- To make visible a new way of living the Gospel today, taking into account man's deep needs and the current historical situation of the Church.
- To open a way. To call to conversion.
- They do not impose themselves. They feel the duty not to destroy anything, to respect everything, presenting the fruit of a Church which renews itself and says to its Father that they have been fruitful, because from them these communities have been born.

How is this mission carried out?

- These communities are born and wish to remain within the parish, with the pastor, to give the signs of faith: love and unity. "Love one another just as I have loved you. By this all men will know that you are my disciples" (Jn 13:34-35). "Father, I in them and you in me, so that they may become perfectly one, so that the world may know that you have sent me" (Jn 17:23). Love in the dimension of the Cross and unity are the signs which create the question marks needed for Jesus Christ to be announced.

The then Archbishop of Madrid came to the end of the *convivence*. He already knew about the experience of the shantytown and had proposed taking the Way to the parishes. On having the reflections which had matured during this *convivence* read to him, the Archbishop began his comments saying, "If I had written this, it would have been the most beautiful page of my life."

Some years later, when the Way had already spread to many parishes in Rome and various dioceses in Italy, the initiators were called to a meeting by the Congregation of Divine Worship which wanted to know what this itinerary for the rediscovery of Baptism consisted of and what rites we were celebrating. The then Secretary of the Congregation, Msgr. Annibale Bugnini, and the group of experts with him, were enormously impressed to see that what they had been working on for some years with regard to the catechumenate for adults – and which would soon be published as the *Ordo Initiationis Christianae Adultorum* (RCIA) – was already being put into action by the Holy Spirit, beginning with the poor. After two years of studying what the communities were doing, a laudatory note *"Praeclarum exemplar"* about the work of the Neocatechumenal Way was published in Latin in the official review of the Congregation (*Notitiae*) for the whole Church. The name "Neocatechumenate" was agreed on with them, to denote an itinerary of post-baptismal Christian formation which follows the guidelines proposed in chapter IV of the *Ordo*. The *Ordo* says, in fact, that some rites proposed by the RCIA for the non-baptized can be adapted also for those who are baptized but not sufficiently catechized.

Along with reciting these salient moments of the history of the Way, its fundamental constitutive characteristic, which is recognized in the *Statute*, should be mentioned: the possibility of living the Christian life in community, recovering the ecclesial model of the first centuries.

Since its beginning, the Neocatechumenal Way has been proposed as a way of initiation to faith: it is not a particular spirituality, but a way of gestation: "*an itinerary of Catholic formation, valid for our society and our times*" (John Paul II, *Letter,* "Ogniqualvolta").

It is a process of maturing in faith that rebuilds the Christian community, which becomes a sign for the world and resists the process of secularization. In this *journey* of faith towards the radicalism of Baptism, the Christian community, and the family as its fundamental nucleus, become central. It is within a concrete Christian community that one can have a personal experience of the Christian life which is live and direct. A word is received, the word becomes liturgy, the liturgy grows, little by little, into *koinonia*, into community. God himself is community of persons.

The gifts of the Spirit which have characterized the development of the Way are many: in particular, the itinerant catechists, the families in mission, the *Redemptoris Mater* seminaries.

Several Bishops, concerned about the situation of secularization plaguing many parishes and seeing that in those parishes where the Neocatechumenal Way had been born small living communities were formed, full of people who had been far away from the Church, asked for the opportunity to open the same way of Christian initiation and requested catechists from other cities or nations. This gave rise to the birth of the *itinerant catechists*. In the meetings of the catechists these requests of the Bishops are made known and those who feel called to depart to announce the Gospel are freely invited to make themselves available for this mission, on the basis of the mandate given by their Baptism. So once again there appears a model of the primitive Church, evangelized by itinerant apostles and catechists, without these forming any special group. They remain inserted in their own communities and parishes, from which they depart and to which periodically they return.

Thus, gradually, through experience and in many *convivences* of formation, itinerant teams for the evangelization have been formed. They are made up of celibate women and men, or couples, and a priest who has the permission of his Bishop or religious superior. For a period these go to another diocese, in agreement with the Bishop who calls them, to open the Neocatechumenal Way in the parishes. This structure of evangelization, which is like scaffolding, is coördinated by the Responsible Team of the Neocatechumenal Way, composed of the initiators, Kiko and Carmen, and a presbyter, F. Mario Pezzi. Over a period of more than 30 years the Way has spread throughout the five continents.

In the face of the situation of northern Europe, where the process of secularization has been going on for many years, the Church is becoming smaller and finds itself in a situation of extreme weakness; above all, the family is destroyed. Inspired by the words of the Holy Father, Kiko and Carmen saw the need to send *families in mission,* both to found the Church in certain zones of *terra nullius,* as an *implantatio Ecclesiae,* and to help reinforce existing communities with families who make visible what a "Christian family" is.

In South America, due to the massive migration from the countryside to the outskirts of the big cities and the scarcity of clergy to open new parishes, these enormous urban agglomerations have fallen prey to the sects. The Bishops, seeing the strength that the Way has to evangelize, asked for families to be sent to these areas on the periphery of the cities – often immense slums – to form nuclei of evangelization which are able to contain the sects by forming small communities, until priests can be sent and new parishes founded.

In 1988 these factors resulted in the sending forth by the Holy Father, John Paul II, the first hundred families to many dioceses where Bishops had asked for them.

These families, who remain united to their own Neocatechumenal Community inserted in the parish, are supported by this community and by the parish for their travel expenses, the renting of houses, the building of new churches, moral support, letters and prayers, etc. In this way a beneficial collaboration between community, parish and mission is born.

The work of evangelization begun by families in different areas very soon showed the need for presbyters to support the new communities which were formed and which would eventually constitute new parishes.

And so in this context the *Redemptoris Mater* Seminaries were born, thanks to the prophetic vision of the initiators of the Way, the courage of Pope John Paul II and the missionary thrust of the families in mission – almost all of them with many children. The witness of faith of these families has been fundamental for re-evangelization and for the formation of new parishes.

These seminaries are *diocesan*: erected by Bishops in agreement with the international Responsible Team of the Way and governed according to the current norms for the formation and incardination of the diocesan clergy. They are *missionary*: the presbyters formed in them are ready to be sent by the Bishop to any part of the world. They are *international*: the seminarians come from different countries and continents, as a concrete sign both of catholicity and of their readiness to be sent anywhere.

Yet the most significant aspect of these seminaries is that, on the one hand, they are a gift which helps the diocese to open itself to mission and go to the whole world; on the other hand, they find in the Neocatechumenal Way a support which accompanies the seminarians throughout the time of their preparation and which continues to sustain them in their permanent formation once they have become presbyters.

10

Canonical Observations on the *Statute of the Neocatechumenal Way*
by Prof. Juan Ignacio Arrieta

By a Decree of the Pontifical Council for the Laity, the *Statute of the Neocatechumenal Way* was approved on June 29, 2002, bringing to a close an interesting process of institutional reflection on the reality of the Way. This came about due to the encouragement and blessing of his Holiness John Paul II, who some time ago requested that this work be finished so the Neocatechumenal could receive a juridical expression within the law of the Church which conformed to the apostolic reality which this Way represents.

As noted, it was the Pope himself who in his letter of April 5, 2001, to Cardinal James Stafford, President of the Pontifical Council for the Laity, entrusted to that Dicastery of the Roman Curia the work of bringing to a conclusion the process of juridical approval of the *Statute of the Way*. By doing so he assigned to this Dicastery the necessary competence in relation to other interested Dicasteries of the Curia.

The drafting of the *Statute of the Way* was concluded, therefore, in close dialogue and collaboration between the Pontifical Council for the Laity and the responsibles of the Way. The final text was approved thus by this Dicastery which in this way was exercising the mandate given by the Holy Father. In the same letter to Cardinal Stafford, the Pope expressed his wish that, once the *Statute* was approved, even if in this case it was not a question of an international association of the faithful, it would be the role of the Pontifical Council for the Laity, as distinct from other organisms of the Holy See, to continue to accompany the apostolic activity of the Neocatechumenal Way.

The text of the document approved *ad experimentum* for a five year period – an elementary prudence normally employed by the Holy See when giving juridical approval to whatever kind of institution – clearly shows that the principal task accomplished during these years of work on the *Statute* has been that of reflecting, in an orderly way and in writing, using juridical terminology, yet with complete fidelity to that concrete experience of Christian life which is the Neocatechumenal Way, in the manner in which it has developed throughout the five continents for the past four decades. The *Statute* is nothing other than the synthetic expression of a reality which already has a life in the Church and they have made present, yet again, the fact – something inevitable, and indeed often necessary, in the life of the Church – that life precedes law. This is why the approval of this *Statute* by the Pontifical Council for the Laity, which acts in the name of the Holy Father, represents above all the confirmation of an apostolic praxis lived and consolidated in recent years.

A *program of formation, not an association*

The *Statute of the Neocatechumenal Way* which has been approved consists of 35 articles divided into 6 sections, plus a final indication regarding the process of revision of the *Statute*. These articles basically describe the principal contents of the catecheses of the Way, the means and times for their transmission, the organization of these catecheses in various stages and relations with the local Church authorities. Attached to the normative body of the text are about a hundred notes which refer above all to texts from Scripture, from the Fathers of the Church or from the Magisterium; texts which in these years have been of fundamental importance in giving shape to the various aspects of this experience of Christian life. It follows that these notes, taken together with the text, are of particular importance for an adequate interpretation of the meaning of the articles which constitute the main body of the

Statute.

In the *Statute* the Neocatechumenal Way is considered to be neither as an association, nor as a movement, nor as a grouping of persons who establish among themselves a special formal link for achieving particular objectives in the Church. Those who know the Way well are aware that none of these categories correspond to the reality of its apostolic experience. Indeed those who are well informed understand that, in this particular case, a canonical option along the lines of an association would have altered the fundamental elements of the Way, compromising essential aspects of its apostolic dynamism. Therefore, rather than describing a juridical entity already codified in the Law of the Church, this *Statute* limits itself to presenting the juridical expression of the reality lived in the Way, obviously in the context of what is stipulated and required by the Church's structure and canonical order.

If we ask, however, what is the concrete juridical form of the Neocatechumenal Way which emerges from this *Statute*, after a careful reading of the document we can quite simply reply that what this text contains is nothing other than "a Neocatechumenal Way." This is what the first article of the *Statute* affirms, using the truly definitive expression of Pope John Paul II in the letter of August 30, 1990, published in *Acta Apostolicae Sedis* (82 [1990] 1515): *"I recognize the Neocatechumenal Way as an itinerary of Catholic formation, valid for our times and society."*

Thus the *Statute* constitutes a kind of Catechetical Directory describing a program or, if you wish, a way of integral Christian formation of a liturgical-catechetical nature, given that it is primarily based on a personal liturgical experience and on a catechetical formation incarnated in the life of the Christian. Furthermore, the *Statute* contains all the fundamental guidelines for organizing, directing and conducting this concrete program of formation – which is offered to every diocesan Bishop who, according to canon law (can. 775, § 1 CIC), is the competent authority for the coördination of initiatives for catechesis in his diocese. At the same time, as a guarantee of the authenticity of the program and the method of formation, and to maintain the necessary contacts with the authority of the Church at different levels, the Holy See entrusts the leadership and the coördination of the activity of the Way to an international responsible team.

From what we have said it can be seen that the *Statute* does not attempt to describe formal elements – new rights and duties, which in reality do not exist – for those who follow this way of formation. Rather, they simply wish to describe the contents that are to be transmitted and the means by which this formation is to be given. There is no need to deny that the Neocatechumenal Way, in fact, clearly consists of a grouping of persons: one has only to think of the small communities formed in parishes which remain substantially stable over time. Nevertheless, it must be emphasized that this phenomenon, in the case of the Way, is not of an associative type. The same thing happens, for example, within the formative structure of a language school or any other educational institution. In these situations there certainly appears a system of stable relations among the students who take courses together over a period of years. However, this does not mean the students establish relationships of a juridical nature among themselves, however intense these human relations may be. On the other hand, for example, in this language school a definite program of teaching has to be followed, those responsible for carrying it out – the professors and the directors of the school – must keep to a methodology already clearly established, accepting the obligations which follow from the respective positions of formation or direction which they occupy.

In the same way, in the itinerary of formation represented by the Neocatechumenal Way, no new juridical relationships are established other than what the faithful have already in virtue of belonging to the Church. Therefore, in the *Statute* no list of rights and duties for those who benefit from this activity will be found. Instead, there is a fairly precise indication of the tasks the catechists, or those who, in complete freedom, make up the various teams of responsibles, must perform. All of this, as mentioned, is a direct consequence of the nature of the Way which in no way corresponds to the characteristics of an association.

The Structure of the Statute

Having said this, we want to describe, in summary form, the content of the approved *Statute*. The first title describes the "Nature and implementation of the Neocatechumenal Way," and is made up of four articles which outline the central organizational aspects of the Way, in keeping with what John Paul II has affirmed on every occasion, regarding the identity of this Christian experience.

The first article informs us that the Neocatechumenal Way is made up of a grouping of spiritual goods—a catechetical itinerary, permanent education, service to the work of catechesis, and so forth, placed at the service of the Bishops as a form of implementation in the diocese of Christian initiation and permanent education in the faith, according to the indications of the Magisterium of the Church. This formation is conducted in the dioceses under the direction of the diocesan Bishop and, obviously, also with the guidance of the international Responsible Team of the Way which the Holy See has indicated as the guarantors before the Church of the identity of this formation.

The second title, "The Neocatechumenate or post-baptismal catechumenate," with its 17 articles distributed over four chapters, forms the central axis on which the *Statute* is based. Here we find a concise and detailed encapsulation of the catechetical content, its formative elements and the timeframe over which this formation is given. Also, the fundamental elements of the Neocatechumenate are described—those for whom it is intended, how it is implemented in the parishes—the beginning of the formative itinerary, its development by means of Word, Liturgy and Community, and a general description of the three different phases which compose the itinerary of formation.

Also described here is the "Initiation and formation to priestly vocation," where we find reference to the *Redemptoris Mater* diocesan seminaries, which is useful for understanding their essential characteristics and their relation with the Neocatechumenal Way. Article 18 begins by quoting a passage from the *General Catechetical Directory* (No. 86) which notes that, like any other catechetical itinerary, the Way is also "a means for awakening vocations to the priesthood and of particular consecration to God in the various forms of religious and apostolic life and for enkindling a special missionary vocation in the hearts of individuals." This is precisely the apostolic context from which the relationship between the Way and the *Redemptoris Mater* seminaries emerges: seminaries are erected at the wish of the respective diocesan Bishops in agreement with the responsibles of the Way, and according to the norms approved by the respective diocesan Bishop, in conformity with the current *Ratio fundamentalis institutionis sacerdotalis*. Thus these diocesan seminaries are for the formation of candidates to the priesthood who are then incardinated for the service of their respective dioceses. Their only unique characteristic is that a specific element of their formative itinerary is participation in the Neocatechumenal Way. It is clear, therefore, that these seminaries must remain marginal to this present *Statute*. In every aspect they come under the universal norms regarding the formation of candidates to the priesthood and the incardination of secular clerics.

The third title examines the collaboration in the renewal of the life of the parish offered by the communities which have finished the itinerary proposed by the Way and which, from that moment, enter a process of permanent education in faith. The fourth title is particularly dedicated to the baptismal catechumenate and to the special care required by catechumens and neophytes.

The fifth and sixth titles of the *Statute* go deeper into the organizational aspects and the forms of service for catechesis. The fifth section, "Forms of service to the work of catechesis" deals principally with those who, in the diocese, who are responsible to follow the activity of the Way. It deals, first with the diocesan Bishop who is the one who authorizes the implementation of the Way in the diocese, watches over it so that the Way develops in accordance with the requirements of Canon Law, presides over the more important rites of the Neocatechumenal itinerary, guaranteeing a reasonable pastoral continuity in the parishes where it is present, etc. The text then deals with the role of the parish pastors and presbyters who exercise the pastoral care of those who follow the Neocatechumenal Way, and who normally are not presbyters formed in the *Redemptoris Mater* seminaries. The text then speaks of the catechists and their formation, of the itinerants-catechists and presbyters-who offer themselves in response to the call of far-off dioceses, and of the "families on mission" who, upon request of the Bishops, establish themselves in de-Christianized areas or places where an *implantatio ecclesiae* is deemed imperative.

Finally, the sixth title contains two articles related to the current composition of the "International Responsible Team of the Way" and to the future substitution of its members by means of election. The responsible team is currently made up of the initiators of the Way-Kiko Argüello, Carmen Hernández and don Mario Pezzi, presbyter of the clergy of the diocese of Rome. The norm provides that, in future, after the death of the initiators, a reasonably large college of people will proceed to elect those who, following confirmation by the Holy See, will assume this function for a period of seven years.

There is also a norm, article 4, which considers the economic aspect of this apostolic activity. It affirms the general principle that the Neocatechumenal Way does not have a patrimony to dispose of, and that it operates in the dioceses by means of services performed on a gratuitous basis; and in response to various necessities, spontaneous collections are made in the communities. The only exception to this rule arises from situations in which apostolic initiatives of greater scope may have to be sustained. Precisely in order to meet these necessities, the diocesan Bishop most directly concerned, upon request of the International Responsible Team, may consider it opportune to erect an autonomous diocesan foundation, with juridical standing, regulated by its own Statutes.

This is thus a basic summary of the content of the *Statute* which have been approved by means of the Decree of the Pontifical Council for the Laity. The Decree and *Statute* are, however, the documents as now published.

Therefore, what the Pope had already indicated in the letter addressed to Cardinal Stafford, quoted above, is now apparent:

namely, that the approval of this *Statute* establishes a clear and sure rule of life for the Neocatechumenal Way and constitutes for it and for the Christian faithful in general, an occasion of profound joy and lively gratitude to God and to the Church. The Pope, making clear reference to No. 30 of the Apostolic Exhortation *Christifideles laici*, concluded that this text constitutes "a new point of departure, which is the visible sign of a mature ecclesial identity."

11

Canonical Observations
by *Dr. Adelchi Chinaglia*[1]

Programmatic Lines of John Paul II

In the speech of the Holy Father to the initiators of the Neocatechumenal Way and the itinerants on January 24, 1977,[2] some basic indications are given for the present *Statute* constituting a new framework in which the Way, even formally, is inserted:

20326. *"The Neocatechumenal Way has completed 30 years of life: the age, I would say, of a certain maturity. Your meeting at Sinai has, in a certain sense, opened before you a new stage."*

20327. *"How can the Neocatechumenal Way be lived in fullness? How can it be developed? How can we share it even more with others? How can it be defended from various dangers...? In order to respond to this question ... you began at Sinai the process of drawing up a Statute of the Way."*

20328. *"It is a very important step which opens the way to the formal juridical recognition on the part of the Church, giving you a further guarantee of the authenticity of your charism.*

The programmatic guidelines indicated by John Paul II affirm that after the substantial recognition given in the letter *Ogniqual-*

---

[1] Head of the legal department of the province of Venice; Doctor in Canon Law.
[2] Cf. *L'Osservatore Romano*, January 25, 1997. For the full text, cf. Appendix III.

volta,³ it is possible to develop (and having matured) those "lines of the initiators," previously recognized as sufficient and valid, into a "Statute of the Way" leading to a "formal juridical recognition," which represents a further guarantee and an answer to the questions posed by the Pope.

This juridical approach is further reconfirmed in the letter of April 5, 2001,⁴ which in the first paragraph speaks of the drafting of a normative Statute in view of its formal juridical recognition and, in point two, that such a recognition consists "in the approval of the Statutes as a clear and secure rule of life."

From these due premises, it follows that:

2034 1. The approval referred to by the Holy Father is the approval of a *Statute* regarding a Catechumenate: more precisely, the approval of the Statutes of the neocatechumenal itinerary or neocatechumenate;

2034 2. Hence it is essential to examine the letter *Ogniqualvolta* since it represents its framework and fundamental presupposition.

The letter *Ogniqualvolta*, besides being a substantial recognition of the Neocatechumenal Way, is also the *Magna Carta* of this form of Christian initiation, considered by the Holy Father as an "*itinerary of Catholic formation, valid for our society and times.*"

This is the thought of the Pope and the underlying "*mens*" of the document:

"*These communities make visible in the parishes the sign of the missionary Church and they open up the way of evangelization to those who have almost abandoned the Christian life, offering them an itinerary of a catechumenal type, which follows all those steps undertaken in the primitive Church by the catechumens before receiving the sacrament of Baptism: it draws them closer to the Church and to*

---

³ John Paul II letter "Ogniqualvolta," August 30, 1990, in AAS 82, 1990, 1513-1515.
⁴ Cf. *L'Osservatore Romano,* April 17, 2001.

Christ" (cf. "Catecumenato Post-battesimale," in *Notitiae* 95-96, 1974, 229).[5]

John Paul II recognizes "the Way" as a post-baptismal catechumenate, supported in this sense by his predecessor Paul VI who, over and over again, expressed himself similarly, affirming a necessity for our age to follow this "*catechumenal itinerary*," going as far as stating that it is "secondary" whether this was done before or after Baptism,[6] thus attempting to apply to the already baptized "a method for their gradual and intensive evangelization, which recalls and renews in a certain way the catechumenate of earlier times."[7]

The letter *Ogniqualvolta* makes three significant statements:

1. The experimentation in time ("after more than 20 years of life of the communities") and the universality of place ("spread throughout the five continents");

2. The implicit confirmation of many pastors and of the Holy Father himself ("*I, too, in the many meetings which I have had as Bishop of Rome in the Roman parishes ... have witnessed copious fruits of personal conversion and fruitful missionary impulse*");

3. The existence of programmatic guidelines able to produce such fruits and indeed producing them, that is, the catechetical-liturgical praxis established and confirmed in various dioceses throughout the world by the relevant pastors, which consists of "*the guidelines proposed by the initiators*," which the Holy Father affirms that he has examined, "*having seen the relevant documentation*" and which he thus explicitly confirms with the key word "*I recognize*" as a fruit of the Holy Spirit, of that same Spirit which *awakens in the Church impulses of a greater fidelity to the Gospel, making spring up new charisms which manifest these realities, and new institutions which put*

---

[5] Cf. John Paul II, letter "*Ogniqualvolta*," Aug. 30, 1990, in AAS 82, 1990, p. 1514.
[6] Cf. Paul VI audience, May 8, 1974, in *Notitiae* 95-96 July-Aug. 1974, p. 230.
[7] Cf. Paul VI, "*Dopo il battesimo*," audience, January 12, 1977, in *L'Osservatore Romano*, January 13, 1977.

them into practice."[8]

Moreover, three years later, in a new document sent to his brothers in the episcopate,[9] "gathered in Vienna to reflect together upon the fruits of the missionary activity which the priests, itinerant catechists and families of the Neocatechumenal Way are producing with generous impulse and great zeal for the Gospel, the Holy Father confirms that the Neocatechumenal Way must be considered as a fruit of the Holy Spirit and that the results achieved attest not only to its capacity *"to respond to the challenges of secularism, to the diffusion of the sects and the lack of vocations,"* but also that its catechetical-liturgical praxis, *"Word of God and participation in the Eucharist make possible a gradual initiation into the sacred Mysteries, form living cells of the Church, renew the vitality of the parish by means of mature Christians capable of bearing witness to the truth through a radically lived faith."*

The Normative Framework of the Statute

The *Statute*, apart from finding its foundation in the papal documents cited, refers clearly to canons 788 of the Code of Canon Law and 587 of the Eastern Code for those who are not baptized, but are applicable, according to the teaching of Paul VI, to those who have begun, even as baptized, a way of conversion for the deepening and maturation of their Baptism.

In this sense, the general norm of the Catechism of the Catholic Church (n. 1231), establishing that *"by its very nature infant Baptism requires a post-baptismal catechumenate"* explains and obliges the baptized to undertake a post-baptismal catechumenate.

The canon of reference, then, for understanding the normative framework for this *Statute* is can. 788 of the Code of Canon Law and can. 587 of the Eastern Code (perhaps more comprehensible): "Those who wish to be joined to the Church (*coniugere volunt*) are admitted through liturgical ceremonies to the catechumenate *which*

---

[8] Cf. John Paul II letter *"Ogniqualvolta,"* Aug. 30, 1990 in AAS 82, 1990, p. 1514.
[9] Cf. John Paul II letter to the "Venerable brothers in the Episcopate," April 12, 1993.

is not to be a mere exposition of dogmas and precepts, but a formation in the entire Christian life through a necessarily prolonged practice (*et tirocinium debite protractum*). *Par.* 2. Those who are in the catechumenate have the right to be admitted to the liturgy of the Word and other liturgical celebrations not reserved to the faithful [the Eucharist]. *Par.* 3. It belongs to particular law to determine the norms for regulating the catechumenate, determining those which are obligations of the catechumens and which prerogatives are recognized to be theirs."

The novelty of this norm, which is later than the Code of Canon Law, lies in the fact that while in paragraph three of can. 788 the competence "to establish Statutes to regulate the catechumenate" lies with the Episcopal conferences, in the corresponding can. 587 of the Eastern Code the regulation rests with "particular law," that is with the ordinary, in line with the most genuine and "traditional" discipline of the Church which places the Bishop at the center of Christian initiation.

Here it can be seen how the approval of the Holy Father—through the competent Dicastery[10] of the present Statute implies the actuation of these canons, offering to the pastors of the universal Church an instrument for the implementation of the general norm provided for by n. 1229 of the *Catechism of the Catholic Church* and, prior to that, n. 64 of *Sacrosanctum Concilium* and n. 14.1 of the Decree *Ad Gentes*.

It is useful to re-read n. 1229 of the *Catechism* to understand the relevance of this "itinerary" and see how it responds to the concern of the pastors for contemporary man, who lives in a context quite similar to that of the primitive Church: "*From the time of the Apostles, becoming a Christian has been accomplished by a journey and initiation in several stages. This journey can be covered rapidly or slowly, certain essential elements will always have to be present: proclamation of the Word, acceptance of the Gospel entailing conversion, profession of faith, Baptism itself, the outpouring of the*

---

[10] Cf. John Paul II letter to "The venerable brother James Francis Stafford," in *L'Osservatore Romano,* April 17, 2001.

Holy Spirit, and admission to Eucharistic communion."

The council restored the catechumenate for adults, divided in various steps, to the whole Church: *"The catechumenate for adults, comprising several distinct steps, is to be restored and brought into use at the discretion of the local ordinary. By this means, the time of the catechumenate, which is intended as a period of suitable instruction, may be sanctified by sacred rites to be celebrated at successive intervals of time"* (SC, n. 64).

On the other hand, the same Code of Canon Law requires in can. 851 n. 1 that *"the adult who intends to receive Baptism is to be admitted first to the catechumenate..."* and canon 865 adds, *"To be admitted to Baptism, an adult must have manifested the intention to receive Baptism, must be adequately instructed in the truths of the faith and in the duties of a Christian and tested in the Christian life over the course of the catechumenate."*

With this "formal" approval, the Holy Father (through the President of the Pontifical Council for the Laity to whom he gives an express and specific mandate with his letter of April 5, 2001), in line with his decree of 1990, offers to the entire Church this instrument, new in its fruits and experimentation, which was born with Kiko Argüello and Carmen Hernández through their experience in the shantytowns of Madrid, rooted in the Second Vatican Council, a post-baptismal itinerary of a catechumenal nature, a valid method for bringing to maturity the faith of whichever baptized or non-baptized person "who manifests the will to embrace faith in Christ" (can. 788) or "to become Christian".

We should not be surprised that history, even that of the Church, repeats itself through analogous situations: after a century of great opulence such as that of the 1500s, and in the face of the need to dialogue with the man of the Renaissance and of the challenge of Protestantism, Paul III did not hesitate (by an *ad hoc* bull) to approve "the Exercises of Saint Ignatius," defined by Pius IX as *"a very wise and universal code for the spiritual direction of souls"* (Fliche-Martin, Vol. XVII, p. 89). In this way he established an original juridical method to safeguard that first *"ordo"* for conversion and growth in faith.

The *Statute of the Neocatechumenal Way* is a new itinerary of Christian initiation, based on a catechetical-liturgical praxis, which has as its principal subject the pastor of the diocese, who is thus carrying out one of the most basic functions, if not the most basic, of the Church. Since this itinerary aims at rebirth in Christ, at his Body, it cannot have any other subject, as source and reference, than the Bishop who thus finds, in the guidelines of the initiators collected in the *Statute*, a norm for the implementation of this type of catechumenate

This is the answer which fulfills the wish of the Holy Father at the Symposium of Bishops of Europe in 1985: there is a need to return to the primitive scheme of the Church, to the origins,[11] "to a true initiation to the mystery of salvation, an integral formation to the Christian life" (*Ad Gentes* 14:1).

Rome, June 2002

---

[11] John Paul II address to the Symposium of European Bishops, n. 13, Oct. 11, 1985.

12

The Rediscovery of the Catechumenate and the Approval of the Neocatechumenal Way
by Giuseppe Gennarini

In order to understand the significance of the *Statute of the Neocatechumenal Way*, it is necessary to look back at some fundamental historical stages which preceded it.

Wojtyla and the Rediscovery of the Catechumenate

Karol Wojtyla, because of his personal experience under a Nazi dictatorship and then later under Communism, sees the Church surrounded by a new wave of paganism expressed in the totalitarian ideologies of the 20th century. In many speeches and acts of his pontificate, one hears an echo of his historical memory of that *realized apocalypse*, experienced in his very person, which was the tragedy of the Second World War, the camps, the gulags, the millions of deaths, the terrible injustices:

> In the course of this century which is coming to an end, young people like yourselves were called together in vast gatherings to learn how to hate. They were sent to fight against each other. The various secularized messianisms, which attempted to take the place of Christian hope, revealed themselves to be true hells.[1]

---

[1] XV World Youth Day, "Vigil of Prayer," presided over by the Holy Father John Paul II, Tor Vergata, August 19, 2000.

The Church and Christians today are called to respond to the danger of a new barbarism, which is far more dangerous than the former ones. For Wojtyla, to re-evangelize means to drive away the specter of a new apocalypse that risks destroying man and society.

Through his philosophical formation, he is alert to real *phenomena* and hence to the fact that faith, if it wants to be Christian faith, must express not only a religious creed, but a new form of life, a new way of loving and of being free. At the heart of the pontificate of John Paul II lies the vision of a Church which, leaving behind all triumphalism, animates a drive for evangelization, a *new evangelization*, in order to re-evangelize traditionally Christian nations which are plummeting into paganism.

In 1952 Wojtyla, a young priest, wrote an article entitled "Catechumenate of the 20th Century," which is extraordinarily relevant today.[2] Reflecting on the Paschal Vigil, he examines the signs which express the Resurrection of Christ: the light that shines from the Resurrection and allows contemplation of the new life and the water, the passage of the Red Sea, symbol of the passage from death to life. This is why at the center of the night there is Baptism, which is the offer of a change of nature prepared by the catechumenate:

> *Tonight the catechumens must be born again.... Can one who is already alive be born again perhaps? Maybe a life can exist which one has not lived up to now?... Because to believe in the God whom Christ announces as his Father ... is not only to believe, but to be reborn again;... we know that ... we do not only belong to a confession, a religion, but that we receive a new life.*[3]

One of the Council Fathers who contributed most to the rediscovery of Christian initiation and hence of the catechumenate was a young Polish Bishop, then auxiliary of Krakow, Karol Wojtyla. In his intervention at the conciliar hall in 1962, during the

---

[2] Karol Wojtyla, "So That Christ May Use Us: Catechumenate of the 20th Century," in *Znak,* Krakow, n. 34, 1952, pp. 402-413.
[3] Ibid.

discussion on the text of the Constitution *Sacrosanctum Concilium* on the liturgy, Wojtyla supported these which at that time were revolutionary:

> *Christian initiation is done not with Baptism alone, but through a catechumenate during which the adult person is prepared to lead his life as a Christian. It is, therefore, clear that initiation is something more than the reception of Baptism alone.*

For Wojtyla, this rediscovery of the catechumenate which broadened the traditional concept of Christian initiation was of

> *the greatest importance above all in our age, when even people already baptized are not sufficiently initiated into the full truth of Christian life.*[4]

As a witness of the faith of the Polish Church, Wojtyla saw with clarity the fragility of "*Christianity*" in front of the secularization and apostasy of modern man.

> *Certainly, we today, in those countries of ancient Christian tradition, especially in the countries of Europe, are being warned of the exhaustion of our interior Christianity, of that which should be the fruit of our Baptism.*
>
> *We are living in a period of de-Christianization; it seems that believers—those once baptized—are not sufficiently mature to oppose secularization, the ideologies which are contrary not only to the Church, to Catholic religion, but contrary to religions in general; they are atheistic, even anti-theistic.*[5]

Wojtyla stressed two profoundly new concepts:

1. The catechumenate is not simply a *doctrinal catechesis*, (as the preparation for Baptism tended to be seen at that time), but an existential process of insertion in the new nature of Christ.

2. The catechumenate, that is the *process which prepared for Baptism*, was as essential to the process of initiation as the sacrament itself.

---

[4] Cf. *Acta Syn.* 1/2, 315.
[5] Cf. "Meeting with the Neocatechumenal Communities in the Parish of Santa Maria Goretti," *L'Osservatore Romano* 1-2 Jan, 1988.

By analyzing the primitive Church, Wojtyla thus saw that at the center of evangelization lay personal witness and the catechumenate. Precisely because she found herself again in a pagan world, the Church needed to recuperate the catechumenate, which in the primitive Church was the drive behind evangelization.

The Reintroduction of the Neocatechumenal Process for the Baptized

At the end of the conciliar discussion on the Constitution for the Liturgy, one of the most important decisions of the Council was precisely that – perhaps somewhat ignored at the time – of reintroducing the catechumenate for adults as a process of gestation for the gradual reception of a new life.[6] This decision led some years later, in 1972, to the promulgation of the *Ordo Initiations Christianae Adultorum* (RCIA), which is the *Ordo*, or schema, which regulates the process of initiation for the Baptism of adults.

Chapter IV of the RCIA also proposes the use of some rites, which belong to the catechumenate, for the catechesis of adults who are baptized but not sufficiently catechized.

In the succeeding years, this concept, still not at the forefront, began to occupy increasingly the center of magisterial documents.

In 1975, Paul VI in paragraph 44 his apostolic exhortation *Evangelii Nuntiandi* concluded:

> It is now beyond any doubt that modern conditions render ever more urgent the need for catechetical instruction to be given under the form of a catechumenate.

Then in 1979, John Paul II in paragraph 44 of his apostolic exhortation *Catechesi Tradendae* stated:

> Our pastoral and missionary concern ... reaches to those who, even though born in a Christian country, indeed in a sociologically Christian context, have never been educated in their faith and, as adults, are true catechumens.

Finally, the *Catechism of the Catholic Church* published in 1992

---

[6] *Sacrosanctum Concilium*, n. 64.

explicitly formulated in paragraph 1231 the need of a post-baptismal catechumenate for all the baptized:

> By its very nature the Baptism of infants requires a post-baptismal catechumenate. It is not only a question of instruction after Baptism, but of the necessary development of baptismal grace in the growth of the person.

In the space of a few years, there has been a progression from Chapter IV of the RCIA, which merely suggested the possible use of some parts of the catechumenate for adults already baptized but not sufficiently catechized, to a formulation which establishes the necessity of a post-baptismal catechumenate for all the baptized.

Not only has the Magisterium welcomed the ideas expressed by Wojtyla as a young priest and then in the Council hall, but the reintroduction of the catechumenate for the baptized has led to the formulation of the need for already baptized Christians to rediscover the faith through a catechumenal itinerary, so as to be ready to confront the challenges of today.

In this way, a document that reintroduced a process for the Baptism of pagans that had been forgotten for centuries, can be seen as being central to the life of the baptized.

The Neocatechumenal Way – Fruit of the Second Vatican Council

While Wojtyla and the Council, and then the Magisterium, were rediscovering the centrality of the catechumenate in the process of evangelization for the non-baptized and also, in a certain way, of the baptized, in a shantytown on the periphery of Madrid, a concrete experience of a post-baptismal catechumenate was developing, thanks to the encounter between Kiko Argüello and Carmen Hernández.

After an existential crisis and conversion, Kiko Argüello, a Spanish artist, discovered in the suffering of the innocent the mystery of Christ crucified, present in the last ones of the world. This led him to leave everything and, following in the footsteps of Charles de Foucauld, to go and live among the poor in the slum of Palomeras Altas, on the outskirts of Madrid.

Another Spaniard, Carmen Hernández, a graduate in chemistry, had been in contact with the renewal of the Second Vatican Council through Msgr. P. Farnés Scherer (a liturgist). She, too, went to live in the slums of Palomeras Altas where she wanted to form a group to go and evangelize the miners of Oruro (Bolivia) and where she met Kiko Argüello.

The encounter in this environment of the very poor between the artistic temperament of Kiko, with his existential experience and his training as a "Cursillos de Christianidad" catechist, and the evangelization zeal of Carmen, who had been prepared at the "Misioneras de Cristo Jesus" Institute and had received her license in theology which gave her knowledge of the paschal mystery and the liturgical renewal of the Council, constituted the *humus,* the *laboratory,* which gave rise to a kerygmatic theological-catechetical synthesis that became the backbone of this process of evangelization for adults – the Neocatechumenal Way.

As a result of their collaboration, there began to take shape an itinerary of formation of a catechumenal type.

This rediscovery in a concrete form of a post-baptismal catechumenate came to the attention of the hierarchy, first through the Archbishop of Madrid, Mons. Casimiro Morcillo who, on coming to the shantytowns, discerned the action of the Holy Spirit and blessed it, seeing in it the fulfillment of the Council – in which he had participated as one of the general secretaries.

Then, in 1972, the Neocatechumenate was studied in depth by the *Congregation for Divine Worship,* which was in the process of publishing the RCIA.

The then Secretary of the Congregation, Msgr. Annibale Bugnini, and a group of experts with him, were impressed seeing that what they had been elaborating for years on the subject of the catechumenate for adults,[7] was already being put into practice by

---

[7] Cf. A. Bugnini, *La Riforma Liturgica,* p. 579, n. 26: "A seriously committed group, that of the Neocatechumenal communities, had already started, through the work of its founders, to lay down a Christian formation for the baptized.... The merit of this group is that they have understood the importance of the spirit of the catechumenate in the formation of true Christians."

the Holy Spirit, starting with the poor. After two years of studying the liturgical-catechetical praxis of the Neocatechumenal Way, they published in *Notitiae*,[8] the official journal of the Congregation, a note praising the work which the Neocatechumenal Way was doing in the parishes, recognizing the Way as a gift of the Holy Spirit for implementing the vision of the Council. Together with the Congregation, the name was agreed upon: *Neocatechumenate* or the *Neocatechumenal Way*.

In 1974, ten years after the birth of the Way, Pope Paul VI gave an audience to Kiko, Carmen and F. Mario along with other pastors and catechists gathered in Rome. In the face of some accusations which raised suspicions of *Anabaptism*, or of the wish to repeat Baptism, the Pope responded with great strength and clarity:

> *To live and to promote this awakening is what you call a new form of "after Baptism" which will be able to renew in today's Christian communities those fruits of maturity and of deepening which in the early Church were achieved by the period of preparation before Baptism. You do it afterwards; whether "before" or "after" is secondary, I would say. The fact is that you aim at the authenticity, at the fullness, at the coherence, at the sincerity of Christian life. And this is a very great merit, I repeat, which consoles us enormously ..."*[9]

The meeting of John Paul II with Kiko and Carmen

On September 5, 1979, John Paul II, who had recently been elected Pope, met Kiko, Carmen[10] and F. Mario personally for the first time, and invited them to a Mass he was celebrating at Castel

---

[8] Cf. n. 95-96, July-August, 1974, pp. 229-230.
[9] Paul VI, general audience, 8.5.74, in *Notitiae* n. 94-96, July-Aug., 1974, p. 230.
[10] The experience of Kiko and Carmen must have awakened in the pope an echo of Albert Chmielowski, a famous Polish painter in the middle of the 19th century, who, after his conversion, reintroduced the painting of religious themes in Poland but then left everything to go and live as "Brother Albert" among the very poor and the homeless as one of them. Chmielowski was a central figure for Wojtyla's vocation and was the protagonist in his play, *"The Brother of Our Lord"* whose theme was the fight of Brother Albert with himself to become a gift for others.

Gandolfo.

The meeting with Kiko and Carmen represented for the Pope a concrete answer to his intuition about the centrality of the catechumenate for the new evangelization. After the Mass, he told them that during the celebration, thinking of them, he had seen "Atheism-Baptism-Catechumenate," thus expressing his conviction that, in the face of atheism, Baptism needed to be rediscovered through a catechumenate.

On November 2, 1980, the first public meeting took place between John Paul II with Kiko, Carmen and F. Mario, in the parish of Canadian Martyrs in Rome. This was the first parish in which, twelve years before, the Way had opened. Speaking to the Neocatechumenal Communities, the Pope said:

> *We are living in a period of radical confrontation which imposes itself everywhere ... faith and anti-faith, Gospel and anti-gospel, Church and anti-church, God and anti-god,... an anti-god cannot exist, but in man there can be created the radical denial of God ... in this our age we need to rediscover a radical faith, radically understood, radically lived and radically fulfilled.... I hope that your experience was born in such a perspective and can lead towards a healthy radicalization of our Christianity, of our faith, towards an authentic evangelical radicalism.*[11]

On January 31, 1988, while meeting with the Neocatechumenal Communities of the parish of Santa Maria Goretti, John Paul II stated with even greater precision the importance of the Neocatechumenate for the Church:

> *Through your way and your experiences you can see what a treasure was for the early Church the catechumenate as a method of preparation for Baptism.... When we study Baptism,... we see more clearly that today's practice has become always more inadequate, superficial ... without a pre-baptismal catechumenate, this practice is not sufficient, it is inadequate for the great mystery of faith and of the love of God which is the sacrament of Baptism.*

---

[11] Cf. *L'Osservatore Romano*, 3-4 November 1980, "Visit to the Parish of Canadian Martyrs."

> *I see here the genesis of the Neocatechumenate: someone—I don't know if it was Kiko or someone else—has questioned himself: Where did the strength of the early Church come from? And where comes the weakness of the Church today which has much bigger numbers? And I believe that he has found the answer in the catechumenate, in this way....*
>
> *There is a way, I think, to rebuild the parish, based on the experience of the Neocatechumenal Way.*"[12]

Here we do not wish to go through all the historical stages which have led to the approval of the *Statute*, which may be read in the Historical Note and Canonical Observations: in particular, the letter *Ogniqualvolta* with which on August 30, 1990, the Holy Father officially recognized the way as an itinerary of Catholic formation. It is necessary only to stress here the approval of the *Statute* as the fulfillment of a long process which has led the Magisterium of the Church to see more and more the need to re-evangelize the baptized and to recognize the Neocatechumenal Way as an instrument valid to this end. Until now, a type of *ordo* or schema which offered a way of putting a *post-baptismal catechumenate* into practice has been lacking.

This is what the Holy See has done with this Decree: it has approved and offered a schema of a post-baptismal catechumenal itinerary, composed, however, not only of liturgical stages, but also integrated with a catechetical content which in more than 30 years has produced numerous fruits.

The recognition of the Neocatechumenal Way is thus one of the concrete realizations of the intentions of the Magisterium and the fulfillment of one of the most urgent needs felt by John Paul II.

---

[12] Cf. "Meeting with the Neocatechumenal Communities in the Parish of Santa Maria Goretti," *L'Osservatore Romano*, 1-2 January 1988.

Appendices

I.

John Paul II: Letter *"Ogniqualvolta"*

TO OUR VENERABLE BROTHER
BISHOP PAUL JOSEF CORDES
VICE-PRESIDENT OF THE PONTIFICAL COUNCIL FOR THE LAITY
APPOINTED "AD PERSONAM" FOR THE APOSTOLATE
OF THE NEOCATECHUMENAL COMMUNITIES

Every time the Holy Spirit causes to germinate in the Church impulses for greater faithfulness to the Gospel, there flourish new charisms which manifest these realities, and new institutions which put them into practice. Thus it was after the Council of Trent and after the Second Vatican Council.

Among the realities generated by the Spirit in our days, figure the Neocatechumenal Communities, initiated by Mr. K. Argüello and Ms. C. Hernández (Madrid, Spain), the effectiveness of which for the renewal of Christian life was acclaimed by my predecessor, Paul VI, as a fruit of the Council: "How much joy and how much hope you give us by your presence and by your activity....To live and to promote this re-awakening is what you call a way "after Baptism," which will be able to renew in today's Christian communities those effects of maturity and deepening that, in the primitive Church, were realized by the period of preparation for Baptism (Paul VI to the Neocatechumenal Communities, general audience, May 8, 1974, in *Notitiae* 96-96, 1974, 230).

I, too, as Bishop of Rome, have been able to verify the copious fruits of personal conversion and fruitful missionary impulse in the many meetings I have had in the Roman parishes with the

Neocatechumenal Communities and their pastors, as well as in my apostolic journeys in many nations.

These communities make visible in the parishes the sign of the missionary Church and they strive to open a way for the evangelization of those who have almost abandoned the Christian life, offering them an itinerary of a catechumenal type which goes through all those stages that the catechumens went through in the primitive Church before receiving the sacrament of Baptism: it brings them back to the Church and to Christ (cf. "Postbaptismal Catechumenate" in *Notitiae* 96-96, 1974, p. 229). The announcement of the Gospel, the witnessing in small communities and the Eucharistic celebration in groups (cf. "Notification on the Celebration of Groups of the Neocatechumenal Way" in *L'Osservatore Romano,* Dec. 24, 1988) is what enables the members to put themselves at the service of the renewal of the Church.

Many brothers in the episcopate have acknowledged the fruits of this "Way." I want only to recall Msgr. Casimiro Morcillo, the then Bishop of Madrid, in whose diocese and under whose governance the Neocatechumenal Communities – which he welcomed with so much love – were born in the year 1964.

After over 20 years of the life of these communities, spread throughout the five continents:

> – taking into account the new vitality which animates the parishes, the missionary impulse and the fruits of conversion which spring from the dedication of the itinerants and, lately, from the work of the families which evangelize in de-Christianized areas of Europe and of the whole world;
> – in consideration of the vocations to the religious life and to the presbyterate which have arisen from this "Way," and of the birth of diocesan colleges of formation to the presbyterate for the new evangelization, such as the *Redemptoris Mater* of Rome;
> – having examined the documentation presented by you:

welcoming the request addressed to me, I acknowledge the Neocatechumenal Way as an itinerary of Catholic formation, valid for our society and for our times.

It is therefore my wish that the brothers in the episcopate – together with their presbyters – value and support this work for the new evangelization so that it may be implemented according to the lines proposed by its initiators, in the spirit of service to the local ordinary and in communion with him in the context of the unity of the local Church and the universal Church.

As a pledge of this desire of mine, I impart to you, and to all those who belong to the Neocatechumenal Communities, my apostolic blessing.

From the Vatican, August 30, 1990, 12th year of my Pontificate.

– JOHN PAUL II

From *L'Osservatore Romano*, English edition, 7, Aug. 14, 2002, p. 4. Italian original in AAS 82 (1990), 1513-1515: *"Epistola R.P.D. Paulo Iosepho Cordes, episcopo tit. Naissitano, delegato "in personam" ad Communitates Novi Catechumenatus.*

II.

John Paul II:
Letter *"È per me motivo"*

TO THE EUROPEAN BISHOPS
MEETING IN A *CONVIVENCE* IN VIENNA

Venerable brothers in the episcopate, dearest brothers and sisters!

It is a cause of great consolation for me, just a few years since my appeal for a new evangelization of Europe, to know that you are gathered in Vienna to reflect together upon the fruits of the missionary activity which the priests, itinerants and families of the Neocatechumenal Way are carrying out with a genuine impulse and great zeal for the Gospel.

On the occasion of the opening of the work of the Special Assembly for Europe on June 5, 1990, I noted with regret that in our continent many people are used to looking upon reality "as if God did not exist." Within such a perspective, I added, man "becomes the source of the moral law, and only those laws which man gives to himself constitute the measure of his conscience and of his behavior" (*Insegnamenti*, vol. XIII, 1, 1990, pp. 1517f). On the other hand, it cannot be denied that the Holy Spirit, by means of the Vatican Council, has raised up valid instruments with which to respond to the questions of contemporary man, and among these is also the Neocatechumenal Way. After various years, having regard to the results which have been achieved, I decided to encourage this experience in writing, in view of the new evangelization, wishing that this experience be helped and valued by my brothers in the episcopate (cf. letter of the Aug. 30, 1990).

Many of you are direct witnesses of such results and also protagonists through the help you have given to spreading this new ecclesial reality; therefore your reflection today is particularly important, as was that of the Bishops of the American continent during the meeting last year in Santo Domingo.

The Neocatechumenal Way, in which the itinerants and the family missionaries mature, is able to respond to the challenge of secularism, the diffusion of sects and the shortage of vocations. The reflection upon the Word of God and the participation in the Eucharist make possible a gradual initiation into the sacred mysteries, to form living cells of the Church and renew the vitality of the parish by means of mature Christians capable of bearing witness to the truth through a radically lived faith. This Way appears particularly qualified to contribute in de-Christianized areas to the necessary *reimplantatio ecclesiae,* leading man in his moral behavior towards obedience to revealed truth and even reconstructing the very fabric of society, which has decayed due to a lack of knowledge of God and his love. Already, in some regions, nuclei of missionary families are being formed which can be the light of Christ and an example of life.

But such a mission would not be possible without presbyters prepared to accompany and sustain with their ordained ministry this work of the new evangelization. I am grateful to the Lord who has willed to raise up numerous vocations and therefore the setting up of the diocesan and missionary seminaries in various countries of Europe, called by the sweet name of the Virgin Mary, *Redemptoris Mater.*

I also place your meeting under her maternal protection and her powerful inspiration, that it may give you further impetus and courage in your apostolic commitment towards contemporary man, who needs the guidance of pastors and of witnesses sent by them, in order to know God, to invoke his name and to receive salvation from him.

May the light of the Risen Lord, which we have solemnly celebrated in the Paschal Vigil, continue to shine within you, sustaining you in your mission in the service of the Church and of the whole of humanity.

From the Vatican, April 12, 1993. John Paul II *(Translation from the original in Italian)*

III.

John Paul II:
"Called to a Special Missionary Commitment"

ADDRESS TO THE INITIATORS OF THE
NEOCATECHUMENAL WAY AND THE ITINERANT CATECHISTS

Dear Brothers and Sisters,

1. Welcome to the Pope's home! I greet you with affection, dear itinerant lay people and priests, together with your leaders who promote the Neocatechumenal Way. Your visit today is a great comfort to me.

I know that you have come directly from your meeting on Mount Sinai and the shores of the Red Sea. For various reasons this has been an historic moment for you. For your spiritual retreat, you chose a place highly significant in the history of salvation, one very appropriate for listening to and meditating on the Word of God, in order better to understand the Lord's plan for you. New evangelization is a fundamental challenge.

This is how you wished to commemorate the 30th anniversary of the Neocatechumenal Way. How far you have come with the Lord's help! In recent years the Way's growth and spread in the Church has been truly impressive. Begun in the slums of Madrid, 30 years later it has become, like the Gospel mustard seed, a great tree which has now spread to more than 100 countries of the world, with a significant presence also among Catholics of the Eastern-rite churches.

2. Like every anniversary, seen in the light of faith, yours, too, becomes an opportunity for praise and thanksgiving for the abundant gifts that in these years the Lord has granted you and,

through you, to the whole Church. For many people the Neocatechumenal experience has been a journey of conversion and maturing in the faith through the rediscovery of Baptism as a true source of life, and of the Eucharist as the culminating moment in Christian life, through the rediscovery of the word of God which, shared in fraternal communion becomes a light and guide for life, through the rediscovery of the Church as an authentic missionary community.

How many young people have also discovered their own priestly or religious vocation thanks to the Way! Your visit today also offers me a happy opportunity to join in your hymn of praise and thanksgiving for the "great things" (*magnalia*) which God is doing in the experience of the Way.

3. Its history belongs to that blossoming of movements and ecclesial groups which is one of the most beautiful fruits of the spiritual renewal begun by the Second Vatican Council. This flourishing was and still is a great gift of the Holy Spirit and a radiant sign of hope on the threshold of the third millennium. Both pastors and lay faithful must be able to welcome this gift with gratitude, but also with a sense of responsibility, keeping in mind that "in the Church, both the institutional and the charismatic aspect, the hierarchy and the associations and movements of the faithful, are coëssential and, although in different ways, contribute to her life, renewal and sanctification" (To participants in the International Colloquium of Ecclesial Movements, *Insegnamenti*, Vol. X/1, 1987, 478).

In today's deeply secularized world, the new evangelization represents a fundamental challenge. The ecclesial movements, which are marked precisely by their missionary zeal, are called to a special commitment in a spirit of communion and collaboration. In the Encyclical *Redemptoris missio* I wrote in this regard: "When these movements humbly seek to become part of the life of local churches and are welcomed by Bishops and priests within diocesan and parish structures, they represent a true gift of God both for the new evangelization and for missionary activity properly so-called. I therefore recommend that they be spread, and that they be used to give fresh energy, especially among young people, to the Christian life" (n. 72). For this reason, for the year 1998, which within the framework of preparation for the Great Jubilee is dedicated to the Holy Spirit, I am hoping for a common witness of all the ecclesial movements, under the guidance of the Pontifical Council for the Laity. It will be a moment of communion and renewed commitment in the service of the church's mission. I am certain that you will not fail to keep this significant appointment. Continue your work in drafting Statutes for the Way.

4. The Neocatechumenal Way is 30 years old – the age, I would say, of a certain maturity. Your meeting at Sinai has, in a certain sense, opened a new stage before you. Therefore you have appropriately sought not only to look back at the past in a spirit of faith, but also to look ahead to the future, asking yourselves what God's plan for the Neocatechumenal Way is at this historic moment. The Lord has put a precious treasure in your hands. How to live it to the full? How to develop it? How to share it with others? How to defend it from various present and future dangers? These are some of the questions you have asked yourselves, as leaders of the Way or as its first itinerants. To answer these questions, in an atmosphere of prayer and deep reflection, at Sinai you began the process of drafting Statutes for the Way. This is a very important step that will lead to its formal juridical recognition by the Church, and it gives you a further guarantee of the authenticity of your charism. As we know, "those who have char ge over the Church should judge the genuineness and proper use (of these charisms) through their office, not, indeed, to extinguish the Spirit, but to test all things and hold fast to what is good" (*Lumen Gentium*, n. 12). I encourage you to continue the work you have begun under the guidance of the Pontifical Council for the Laity, and especially of its Secretary, Bishop Stanislaw Ryłko, present here with you. My special prayers go with you on this path.

Before concluding, I would like to give a Cross to several sisters as a sign of their fidelity to the Church and their total dedication to the evangelizing mission. May the Lord Jesus be your comfort and support at difficult moments. May the Blessed Virgin, mother of the Church, be your model and guide in every circumstance. With these wishes, I impart my affectionate blessing to you here present and to all who are involved in the Neocatechumenal Way.

Translated from *L'Osservatore Romano*, Jan. 25, 1997 (Italian original).

IV.

Letter of John Paul II

TO CARDINAL JAMES FRANCIS STAFFORD

To my Venerable Brother Cardinal James Francis Stafford
President of the Pontifical Council for the Laity

1. Four years have now gone by since that memorable Jan. 24, 1997, when I had the occasion to meet the initiators of the Neocatechumenal Way and, with them, the numerous persons in charge of the communities of the Way throughout the world. On that occasion, joining myself to their prayer of praise and thanksgiving to the Lord for the precious fruits brought by the Way in 30 years of life, I did not fail to emphasize the importance of some unavoidable obligations on which the very existence of the Way depends. Among these, the drafting of precise Statutes in view of its formal juridical acknowledgement (cf. *To the Neocatechumenal Way*, 24 Jan. 1997, n. 6; *L'Osservatore Romano* English edition, 5 Feb. 1997, p. 9). Thus a new stage was begun which was decisive for the future of this ecclesial reality.

2. Already in the Apostolic Exhortation *Christifideles laici* (30 Dec. 1988) I recalled that "no charism dispenses a person from reference and submission to the *Pastors of the Church*" (n. 24), and I referred to what is written in this regard in the Dogmatic Constitution *Lumen gentium:* "Judgement as to their (charisms) genuineness and proper use belongs to those who preside over the Church, and to whose special competence it belongs, not indeed to extinguish the Spirit, but to test all things and hold fast to what is good (cf. 1 Thes 5: 12; 19-21)" (n. 12). It is on this condition, in fact, that charisms, in their diversity and complementarity, can work together for the common good (cf. *Christifideles laici*, n. 24).

This process of recognition and acceptance of charisms is therefore not an easy one. It requires a profound discernment of the will of God and must be accompanied by constant prayer, so that hearts may be readily opened to the voice of the Spirit in ecclesial communion. The climax of this process is the official act of recognition and approval of the Statutes as a clear and sure rule of life, an occasion that the ecclesial communities concerned always live with great joy and sincere gratitude to God and to the Church. The new point of departure is in fact a visible sign of a mature ecclesial identity (cf. *Christifideles laici*, n. 30).

3. I know with how much zeal and pastoral care the Pontifical Council for the Laity strives to accompany the Neocatechumenal Way in this crucial stage of its life: the preparation of the Statutes. I entrusted this delicate task, your Eminence, to this Pontifical Council for the Laity, because of the authority which it holds, on the basis of current canonical regulations, in addition to the special experience that it has in this field. Herein lies the hope of a successful outcome of the procedure, by now heading towards its concluding phase.

While I express to the Pontifical Council for the Laity my sincere appreciation and my gratitude for the seriousness and rigor adopted in the task assigned to them, I confirm its expertise in the approval of the statutes, once they are duly drafted, and I also charge them to continue accompanying the Way in the future. I am sure that in fulfilling this mandate the Pontifical Council for the Laity will be able to count on the coöperation and the spirit of filial docility of the Neocatechumenal Way.

In entrusting to the Lord, through the intercession of Mary, Mother of the Church, the activity of the Council over which you preside, I sincerely impart to you, venerable Brother, as also to your assistants, my affectionate Blessing.

From the Vatican, April 5, 2001

V.

Congregation for Divine Worship
Note on the Neocatechumenal Communities

Omnes reformationes in Ecclesia novos gignerunt inceptus novasque promoverunt instituta, quae optata reformationis ad rem deduxerunt.

Ita evenit post Concilium Tridentinum, nec alter nunc fieri poterat. Instauratio liturgica profunde incidit in vitam Ecclesiae. Spiritualitas liturgica novos germinare flores sanctitatis et gratiae necesse est, ne non **intensioris** *apostolatus catholici et actionis pastoralis.*

Praeclarum exemplar huius renovationis invenitur in "Communitatibus neocatechumenalibus," quae ortum habuerunt Matriti, anno 1962, opera quorumd miuvenum laicorum, Exc.mo Pastore Matritensi, Casimiro Morcillo, permittente, animante et benedicente. "Communitates" eo tendunt ut in paroeciis signum exstent Ecclesiae missionariae, viamque conantur aperire evangeliziationi eorum, qui vitam christianam paene dereliquerunt.

Ad huc finem Sodale "Communitatum" quaerunt vitam liturgicam intensius vivere, incipiendo a nova catechisi et praeparatione "catechumenali" nempe, percurrendo spirituali itinere, omnes illas baptismi acciperent. Cum hic agatur non de baptizandis, sed de baptizatis, catechesis eadem est, sed ritus liturgici aptantur situationi christianorum baptizatorum iuxta suggestiones iam datas a Congregatione pro Culto Divino.

"Communitates" in paroeciis eriguntur, sub moderamine parochi. Sodales semel vel bis in hebdomada coadunantur ad audiendum verbum Dei, ad colloquia spirituali agenda, ad Eucharistiam partecipandam.

OUR TRANSLATION:

All the reforms in the Church have given rise to new initiatives, and have promoted new norms to enable the purposes of the reform to be put into practice.

This was so after the Council of Trent; and it could not be otherwise in our own day. The liturgical renewal penetrates deeply into the life of the Church. Liturgical spirituality must, of necessity, germinate new flowers of sanctity and grace, as well as a more intense Christian apostolate and spiritual action.

An excellent example of this renewal is to be found in the "Neocatechumenal Communities" which arose in Madrid in 1962, through the initiative of some young lay people, with the permission, the encouragement and the blessing of the most excellent pastor of Madrid, Casimiro Morcillo. The communities aim at making visible in the parishes the sign of the missionary Church, and they strive to open the road to evangelization for those who have almost abandoned the Christian life.

To this end, the members of the "Communities" seek to live the Christian liturgical life more intensely, starting with a new catechesis and a "catechumenal" preparation, passing, in a spiritual itinerary, through all those stages which the catechumens in the primitive Church went through before receiving the sacrament of Baptism. Since they are not people awaiting Baptism, but people already baptized, the catechesis is the same, but the liturgical rites are adapted to the conditions of baptized Christians, according to the directives already given by the Congregation for Divine Worship.

The "Communities" in the parishes are set up under the direction of the pastor. The members meet, once or twice a week, to listen to the divine Word, for spiritual dialogue, and to participate in the Eucharist.

Additional copies of this book may be obtained
by contacting
Hope Publishing House
P.O. Box 60008
Pasadena, CA 91116 - U.S.A.
(626) 792-6123 / (800) 326-2671
Fax (626) 792-2121
E-mail: hopepub@sbcglobal.net